T0129631

Authenticity

Cross the bridge to The realities of Life

Noel G. Grace

BALBOA.PRESS
A DIVISION OF HAY HOUSE

Balboa Press books may be ordered through booksellers or by contacting:

Balboa Press
A Division of Hay House
1663 Liberty Drive
Bloomington, IN 47403
www.balboapress.com
1 (877) 407-4847

Scripture taken from the King James Version of the Bible.

Print information available on the last page.

ISBN: 978-1-9822-2791-3 (sc)
ISBN: 978-1-9822-2792-0 (e)

Balboa Press rev. date: 07/02/2020

Contents

Caution

Before you commence this complecated venture, I am persuaded to interject a request on you, not to rush the consumption of the contents of this media as it contains the realities of life. In this world that was made and is sustained by God, it's customary that whenever God is mentioned people are detered. In order to proceed please be reminded that each of us is an indevidually enclosed and timed package. No one is compelled to accept anyother human implicatons or opinions.

Based on the complicated nature of this venture caused by difference in languages and comprehension capabilities of desernment. I've made my request known to the main source of my inspirations for his peace. Thereby I'll utilize the instrument called repitition and anticipate the tolerance of this audience. Happiness is an expensive component of our beings, this commodity is complicated and not easily attained based on the decisions we make. It most certainly is a component of love and satisfaction to nuture our hearts.

This book is dedicated to my doctors Dr Bruce Wishnov and my cardeologist Dr. Bauerlein, they will be spiritually compensated for participating in the perpetuation of my life. I've been taken this far by the hands of the Almighty to forward in this generation triumphantly, please help me sing the redemption song to freedom in paradise. In order to activate your minds the word "it's" will be viral in this venture. Let's proceed!

Preview

Persue the acquisition of wisdom from knowledge by seeking potent substance to desern the right pathway of our predestined life's destination. We were all placed here on this planet earth for a duration of time in order to accomplish a mission for a purpose, so time is of the essence. We are not recycleable, it's a one way endeavor no second chances. Humanity is unique in nature as we are the only specie that have the capabilities we posses and utilize.

Every other living creature require a source to be functional, in the case of us humans money is not a source it is a resource that's derived from different processes. All wealthy humans derive riches from three sources, inheriting it, exchange labor for it or have money work for them in a process called investments. The most important aspect of our being at an early stage in life is getting equipped with education. At this time in existence the three most vital subjects are science, mathematics and literature.

There are times when it is beneficial to be silent as it's spelt with the same letters as listen. Life is a wonderful thing if we make it just that, and no in between. Success is attainable with mental aspirations in conjunction with adjustments to our mental paradigms. One man's fear is another man's fortune, always aim for the gold if you acquire the bronze it's better than nothing. If we knock our minds will open. Our destiny is ruled by God, let's put the rest of our lives in full motion, going forword.

Enjoy the rest of this publication in a timely manner. Do not be detered by me mentioning God in the equation, He is the foundation on which it all stands. Love is a fruit of the Spirit and a vital component of our being, not an action for satisfaction, it's a powerful feeling of compassion to utilize and enjoy in it's season. Love cannot be re-made, God made it and placed it in us and it can be explored to enjoy the power and pleasures of it. Joy is a component of love and it has been identified to come in the morning.

It's like a brilliant bloom of a flower in the dawning of a brand new day. An important aspect of our being is to cultivate love in the garden of our minds to attract other elements like a magnet. Happiness is the bloom of love, it inpliments a complicated monument that penitrates our imagination with pleasure. It was predicted that the lacking of knowledge will cause humanity to perrish, knowledge is acquired from potent literature and life experiences. In this life it's of paramount importance that we make our light shine that others will see our good works and come to expand the kingdom of the Almighty.

Life is a timed and gifted previlage, don't leave earth without experiencing it in it's entirety. Oh how good and pleasant it is for us all to live in peace, love, hormony and unity it's like honey from blossoms to a bee. Today is the first day in the rest of our lives, let us all give thanks to God for sustaining us. When the lightning flash, the thunder roll, the sun shine the rainbow in the skyes and the wind blow, we must realize there is a mighty power behind it all.

Introduction

Presenting the author Noel G. Grace who originated from the caribbean island of Jamaica, an author with the assignment to explore and disclose the true realities of life with guidance to persue it's pathway. As we go along we'll get to know eachother more and I am sure you will not agree with all my views, however you are permitted to desern and ponder them. I will invite you to get with me in the words of our maker, in order to make the necessary preparation for attaining the place being prepared for us in eternity called paradise.

I will disclose that I always endeavor to keep my commitments and one of them is to continue doing my explorations and share them with my readers. I will encourage you to acquire and read my books, "Truly amazing Grace" early 2020 "A visionary Messenger" mid year, and "Authenticity" targeted for late 2020. It is a concept that came to my mind and impacted mental faculties with substance, it's beneficial to humanity. It's not the size of a gun that determins the damage it does, it's the effect of the bullet.

Getting to know me I will declare that I'm a possession of the only true God Jehovah and requested of him that he use me for his purpose that his will be done. I am secured in him and when I leave this life, I'll go to rest in Christ his son and await my resurrection, After the judgement we go to eternal paradise with both Christ and Jesus. I'm not an instigator but my wish is that my endeavors will impact human's minds and they come to expand the kingdom on earth as it is in heaven. Each time we see the rainbow it's a reminder of God's promises.

The joy of the Lord is our strength, may we be empowered by experiencing an aboundance of his joy. History have revealed the magificience of our God. I have been notified by my intellect that it's getting congested with mental substance to be disbursed to my international audience. The financial infrastructure that the religious industry is constructed on is becoming more profotable than the entainment one. Most of the popular actors are getting saved by the bell in Jesus's name with a passport to heaven to follow that money.

It was customary that former things will pass away to be history but in this case it's destined to be resurrected. Mortality will be reinstated to be the order of the the day with excitement to keep the evil adversary happy., Because of the false hope that religions have implanted in human minds of the world. Everyone is deceived and aspire going to heaven to walk the streets of glory. Heaven is a spiritual kingdom of God and the earth is being prepared to be like it on the new cleansed earth called paradise.

I will remind you that his promises are sure, the first cleansing of this earth was with water and the next will be with fire. There will come that moment in time when every knee will bow and every tongue confess that Christ the true son of God and a member of the trinity of God is Lord. Being a visionary messenger, in my research I have identified a default that I will share with you my audience. The teachings of religions have installed a reverse gear in the transmission of human lives.

The bible is being utilized as the main source of directives to substantiate their mission. I have identified my assigned mission and it's designed to direct the minds of humanity in the correct direction to our final destination. I will remind you that it was the same stratigy satan used then as he is now that caused God to distroy the first world with that flood. Because knowledge have increased by inspirations from God, my anticipation is that we the now world will make the right decision by choosing eternal paradise.

There are only two choices, 1. distruction in the lake of fire with satan or 2. being with the Lord and Jesus in iternal paradise, be sure to choose the latter. Lord/God the trinity exist in the realms of glory the secret place of the most high and not in heaven. Satan's religions have humanity worshiping the same false god as in the first world there will be another cleansing but this time it will be by fire. As long as you include that false image of Jesus devised my satan in your worship you are in reverse.

I hope you don't mind me sharing my paragatives with you, 30 years ago I accepted Christ as my Lord and Savior and was submerged under water in the name of the Father, Christ and Holy his spirit. I was saved by grace by faith in Christ, not of works that anyone should boast. Based on my intelligence I followed the precepts specified in the holy scriptures as to my ultimate spiritual destiny and my security in eternal paradise with Christ and Jesus, I hope to encounter ya'll there.

It was a process of persuing and finding the truth and the way to my maker to have intersession with him and I did eventually. I'm now in the process of learning God's will and will always acknowledge him and he will direct my narrow pathway to eternal paradise. I have made the decision to get out of religions because of their devisive agenda and get connected to the truth because the words of God are Truth. The scriptures specify that Christ is God the Word, and Truth, Life and Way.

He was from before the beggining. I will not apologize for sharing my spiritual commitments with you. It does go without saying that the key to it all is love, love God, love yourself and love all others as yourself. It is of vital importance to establish a personal relationship with our maker and sustainer whereby we communicate with him by way of Christ the only way. I'm not affiliated with any religion as 80% of them uses the King James version of the bible whereby the name of our father is replaced with the title Lord.

The title Lord is for the combination of the three spirits of God only, anyone outside of the trinity is secondary and subjected to God the authority. I have acquired the confidence of meeting with Christ and Jesus at the gate of paradise to dwell with them eternally, giving Jahovah our father thanks and praise continually. When Jesus was here on earth he said several times that it was the father that sent him here. May the peace of God that preserves our understanding keep our hearts and mind in Christ.

He will be with those of us that made the right choice of accepting Jesus as our saviour. It is imperative that we make our light shine for others to see our works and join us. I have a friend who's mother passed away recently and she told me that she wish that there was a telephone to call her mom in heaven, she's not there. We are not able to communicate with those that have passed but we can talk to God through our intercessor Christ, and through the power of his Spirit in prayer.

Many religions utilize the misconseption of going to heaven when they die and that's totally misleading. That's not the way it was designed to be, whenever anyone dies if they are a child of God they go to rest in Christ. The others who choose to be satan's possession will go in holding, dont ask me where and awaite resurrection for judgement. Death was appointed to all humans and the mortal remains will be disposed of as dust in the ground or as burnt to ashes in the lake of fire with the evil adversary satan.

Preparation For The Ride

On a regular basis we all should make a joyful noise unto God and come before His presence with singing, in honor and praise. There is no greater name than the name of Jehovah God our father, by way of Christ his son. and Jesus our savior. I do have a following on social media that I share positive substance with on a daily basis, do not be detered by my demeanor and mentioning of God in this publication because he is the sustainaner of our being. Life contains numerous systematic processes and some are critical to the progressive agenda I'm trying to instill in you.

Our mind, heart, and soul are all located in our head and directed by our brains to function normally. There are times when the evil one will intervene and try to deceive us, but the remedy is to equipt our being with words from God. His word is light to our pathway to him. There are also different relationships and friendships some intimate with commitments, oh how sweet and pleasant it is with all the right components. It is essential to utilize the enormous amount of our capabilities and mental assets we possess.

I am not insinuating the culmination of a congestive mindset, beneath the mountains of uncertainties curtailed in time are enormous amount of possibilities. It is good and pleasant for us all to live in peace, love and unity to acquire joy, as the joy of the Lord is our strenght. The bible stipulates that the fear of God is the beginning of wisdom, I consider that misleading as God want us to fear nothing. Like a hen sitting on her eggs in the nest, may our hopes and dreames be achievable in the nest of life. Regardless of the high degree of uncertainties, with positive anticipation, tollerance and persistence our boats will anchor in times of storm.

We are required to acquire positive faith and be optimistic for the accomplishments of our perceptions. Our emotions are essential to our being, we were born crying, there are tears of joy from the heart and tears of sorrow from the mind. We must curtail our emotions as it's possible for them to go out of control and become dangerous enough to cause grief. It is beneficial to prioritize our mental faculties, our beliefs are essential. It is also essential to prioritize our actions based on the anticipated outcome.

Do not rely on our hopes and dreams they have a high degree of uncertainties to impact the anticepated end product. Our deeds have the capability to expose the characteristics of our being, do good and be blessed and compensated accordingly. Meekness is a vital asset for our being, it is specified in the words of God that the meek ones among us will inherit paradise earth, and obtain mercy. I always practice what I preach and that's what I'm doing here with you, if you should get bored or disagree with my views don't be detered just skip the page.

In order to achieve and enjoy the pleasures of life, we must get our priorities in the right sequence. Love is the key element in the process, love and honor our sustainer and it all will fall in place. The true you is not your personality, presentation, attitude, verbal utterances or actions. Your true being is located in your spiritual heart, adjacent to your minds and located in our head. Love is a main component of our being and a fruit of our spirit and should be utilized in actions and emotions accordingly, always try to satisfy the needs of the needy.

I have developed the concept of welcoming each new day with an heart of gold to glow for others to desern it and come to the Lord. The persuit of life is not an easy road, there are rivers to cross, mountains to climb overlooking the valleys and intersections. There are much to be achieved, go get it tiger and bring me some. The bell already rang, this is a wake up call to take action and change from the negative to the positive. Mejority of humans allow themselves to be controlled and monipulated by the system of things.

I will remind you that the adversary is the god of this world and is totally irresponsible in the process of guidance to progress. The ball is totally in our courts, take advantage of the opportunities based on the identification of the defaults, it is of vital importance. Time and time again we read of accounts of rags to riches of real people that took control of their lives and ascended to a higher elevation in existence. It is essential to cultivate aspirations and utilize determination to achieve the goals we set.

In my projects of exploring trends and progress across the globe I have had some suprized experiences whereby large developed countries like China utilize their financial resources to exploit less fortunate ones that possess recources but lack of the technology to acquire them.There are countries with lots of resource and potential like Africa is being exploited by China. The train of life is moving right along one day at a time, make hay while the sun is shineing and seek shelter when it rains.

Carefully persue the pathway of life utilizing our allotment of time based on our predestined blueprint. Never allow the dark clouds of our today to impede the brilliant glow of a brighter tomorrow although it is promised to no one. Our sustainer can is in control of our future and curtail any irregularities aimed at us. Life was not designed to be an easy road it has it's challenges to encounters and endure. Blessed are they that walk not in the council of the ungodly nor sit in the seat of the scornful nor associate with evil, but delight in the laws of Almighty God and meditate on his words day and night.

Those catigories of humanity will be like trees planted by the rivers of water that bring fruits in it's season and whatever they do will prosper. We must all come to the realization that life without it's challenges would have a void, let us all join in the venture with endurance to reach the ultimate destination. It's the desire of the system of things to keep us ignorant by devising distractions to divert our attention. There are systems like politics, religions and others that are devised to infect our minds in this world sending our minds in a state of confusion.

I was assigned to put the pendulum of our conscious minds in motion with substance to ponder with our hearts and minds.

I will encourage you not to rush the reading of this book as there are enormous amount of material to absorb and digest mentally. There will come a time when you will be required to make adjustments to the mental paradimes in order for the process to make the necessary changes in our lives. Because our subconscious minds are unpredictable due to the environmental influences.

The evil spiritual diversions has to be continuous reinforcement using the art of repetuation. All the elements of the equation will be addressed in this book as it's designed to be a life manual for reference. If at anytime you feel like going out of your comfort zone, flip the page and go back to the index. Choose a subject, penetrate the contents of it in order to enjoy your investment. There will be moments when issues seem unreal, sit back relax and enjoy the experience.

There will be treats and humor, pleasure and pain with food for the brain, pick your choice and enjoy the ride. Hearts will be activated in sequence of the process, one will be pondering while the other pump blood through our bodys. It is benificial to make time to cultivate productive thoughts as everything in existence except the elements of nature created by God was obtained from a thought. There will come a time when it will seem controversial, that is great as controversy generates clarity.

This information is designed to be a new awakening to realize the true realities of life and make the necessary preparations by getting our conscious minds in motion. It is of vital importance to introduce this book containing all this information to all your friends family and associates to get them involved. This would seem like commencing a revolution, no its not, instead it is an evolution in preparation for our final destination. Controversy activates curiosity and eventually alleviates boredom, there is no perfection in civilization.

There will be times with incidents of imperfection and might interupt the process of this dialogue. We humans are uniquely constructed with elements like desires, attractions, motivations, likenesses, preferences, perceptions, moods and several others. Most people are out there somewhere lost in an illusion and will not come to the realization of the realities of life, that's an unfortunate circumstance as they eventually end up in desperation. Because that evil adversary have access to our minds even in our sleep he will intercept with deceptive dreams.

The holy history book was designed as a manual for life as it contains words from God through the mouths of humans including Jesus when he was and can be diverted to high altitudes to substantiate almost any concept or beliefs. A friend of mine just discovered that I'm an author and enquirer of the subjects I indulge in and started a conversation that hit me like a bullet. I always go by the accounts recorded in the scriptures whereby it disclosed that God made Eve from components of Adam that's incorrect. Adam was created with a female mate name Lilleth the only two created humans.

Eve the companion of Adam was made by God from dust

of the earth. I will confess to you that based on my research I discovered that a portion of Adan's mental faculties was implanted in Eve. That's why ever since that procedure all males are seen as mentally incomplete. As a matter of fact the only time a male's mind experience completeness is after the process of copulation. And that's why they have a tendency of falling asleep after that act. Emancipate yourselves from mental slavery, none but ourselves can heal our minds.

Have no fear for atomic energy because none of us can stop the predestined and timed process. The predictions in the book of Ezekiel must be fulfilled and the kingdom of mistry Babylon the great will fall. They keep eradicating our prophets and all we can do is to excercise tolerance. Let's join together and sing a redemption song to freedom. Most of the preceeding substance was stipulated by Robert Nesta Marley a Jamaican prophet in reggae music, legend and hero.

Based on the sequence of events scheduled for the ending of time, the begginning of the end have begin by America firing the first missile that eradicated two dignitaries in Iran. It will be a while to go and there will be weeping, mourning and gnashing of teeth. This is the year 2020 and presently there are massive actions of nature in parts of this earth. There are also roumers of war which are signs that were predicted. When the time comes, Babylon will be the prime target for destruction and the detrimental distructive missile will be fired by Russia.

Presently China is demolishing churches and synigogues and persecuting religions and christianity. In Japan is likewise people have to be worshiping in caves and other hiding places. The main commodity religions have up for sale is a blue eyed cocation image of a man they named Jesus. Mary was a brown skin woman with curly hair, no one have ever seen God but the seed was inplanted in Mary by Holy his spirit was from Christ. Christ is the Word and member of the trinity of God with no begginning or end.

Religions that were devised and implimented by the evil adversary will deceive you otherwise causing you to have a mark of the beast. The good thing is you do have the previlage to make the right choice and seek the Lord while he can be found. Recently the Roman Chatholic pope, the highest monarchy in that religion announced that homosexuailty is now legal and was seen kissing another male associate calling for peace among all nations. This is a reminder of Sadom and Gomaro, there will be no peace as the evil adversary have ignited the flame for his purpose.

The preceeding disclosure is a total abomination to God, and is sinful, the bible stipulates that God hates sinful acts whereby the wages of sin is death but the gift of God to us humans is eternal life in paradise with Christ and Jesus his representetive for whoever chooses that pathway. Rejoice I say rejoice and give thanks to Almighty God for sustaining us with all our requirements for survival. I am appealing to you again, do not be detered from enjoying your investment in purchasing this book.

What I'm trying to instill in you are realities of this life we encounter consistently, things may be different in other parts of this world but I'm speaking from an American point of view in english. Laughter and tears are both international displays of joy in our minds. Tears is liquidation of our emotions and the most versetile as there are tears of joy and tears of sorrow. It can be discribed as a liquid state of mind and there are moments when degrees of laughter get intence enough to liquify the demeanor with tears.

There are different sounds associated with both responces but laughter is more vibrant whereby it can activate other body functions. There are unique body functions that can be catigorized as moments of solidarity for our beings.We were given the previlage of living life to the fullest based on our choices and decisions, it's in our best interest to love eachother and give thanks and praise to our sustainer continually. In recent times people go beyond their means and end up having stressful lives.

It's better to stay within means and keep a song of joy in our minds, the joy of the Lord is our strength you don't have to sing it out loud just hum. It's always fun to sing in the shower, never allow other people's moods and attitudes to disturb your peace. May we all as a body called the world, taste and see that the Lord God is good and his mercies endures everlasting. It's benificial to make a commitment to continually give God thanks and praise in aboundance.

I'm aware that there are hatehiests out there and welcome them into the fold, if not they'll be posessions of the evil adversary destined for distruction in the lake of fire. Us all humans are individually made as a unit with the mental capability of desernment and comphrention to make the right decisions and choices. Lack of wisdon from knowledge create vulnerability to cause default in the equasion of survival. If we make wrong choices or decisions we'll suffer the consequences and if we make the right ones we'll reap the benifits.

Any action we take in words or deeds has a reaction to encounter, credibility is a vital element in getting compensated. We should always make sure that the words we utter are truthful and credible, always endeavor that the commitments we make are kept safely. If for any reason you acquire a loan, be sure you repay it according to hits terms. Always endeavor to choose compliance over complecations as the latter can be in a problematic packege.

At this time in the persuit of my life there's nothing more substantial than exploring the source of my existence. I'm convinced that God is utilizing me for a purpose. Based on the inspirations being implanted in my mind, I'm presently at a point where my curiosity is going wild as my exploration for facts have intensefied. It's my intent to continually sharing my findings with my international audience.

Ofcourse I must find ways to have the substance of this venture by ways of translelation in different languages. It's of utmost importance to make spiritual medetations a daily routine. The most complicated limb of a human's body is the head, it contains the main control center of our entire functions in existence. Consisting of two minds, one heart, five sences and one brain. Over the years there has been a population explosion that make it difficult for them to keep up with the demand for foods.

At this moment in time 2020 America have developed a mean by paying millions of dollors from the taxpayers money to a laborotary in China to create a bacteria calling it a virus and named it covid 19. The force behind it all is the god of lies, the evil adversary satan. This was devised to be an investment involving several billionaires and the two main purposes are to reduce the population of the world from seven billion to fifty five million, that's a lot of lives with souls that are precious to God. The second plan is to insert the mark of that beast in the world of humanity as disclosed in the bible.

Here in the western hemisphare to keep up with the growth they have resorted to fast foods and heavily chemically processed ones too. Another poisonous factor is what we drink, the most popular drinks are soda pops and they are totally poisonous to our body functions. It have been reported that Japan has the highest rate of survival in the world because of the food they consume, they eat less fast and processed foods and red meat. What they consume are mostly sea foods and vegetables, less coffee and more teas. whenever the human body is malnurished, the resistance rate becomes too low to counteract infections.

It's what we absorb into our bodies that causes deseases and illnesses, but it's all like fuel to a multi-billion dollar industry known as medication otherwise called drugs. The demand has gotten to the point that a large percentage of the medications are now being made overseas and called generics. If you are observant you'll see on most intersections in US cities there are monument built for drug distribution and in some cases across from eachother with different names.

No wonder there are so many sick people around, they are created by the system for the system, the healthcare industry and their share holders are laughing straight to the bank. We are trapped because if we decide to go vegetarian we still are at a disadvantage as the vegetables are produced with chemical fertilizers in order to keep up with the demand. Another area is drinking water, most drinking water is derived from pumping wells, stored in metal tanks and have to go through a process before it gets in the pipes to our homes. They sell distilled water also for human consumption.

The water does go through a chemical process all we need is filtered spring water. Our bodies do require a substantial amount of water for the filtration process in the function of our bodies. Writing a book is fun and rewarding similar to listening good music, usually there are very touching messages in the lyrics of music that impacts the mind with comfort and entertainment. The difference is to be able to acquire knowledge, information and directives from potent literature.

To substantiate this perception as an author because it put my mental faculties to work. My advice to all humanity worldwide is to acquire knowledge and equipt their being with wisdom to be successful. My main purpose here is to acquire information by way of inspiration and share it here and on social media to benifit humanity and motivate your minds. It's essential to utilize our tallents, there are people that use their voices to make joyful noises for entertaining human minds.

There are others that document their asperations in literature. There are numerous trends to identify and excell to be recognized and derive fame and fortune. I will complement you for choosing to be in this environment to acquire fertilization for your minds. This is an environment that's fantaticy free so it's benificial for the development and preservation of your minds.The human body was designed to function in a state of vacuum, the only time it's otherwise is when it's in a dump mode to discharge waste.

Seasons comes and goes, because the earth rotates on it's axis and the sun is stationary. Nature is truly amazing and it produces a lot of natural resources to sustain humanity. A factual and peculiar matter is that the planet known as the sun does not rotate like the earth does but have great impact on all the other planets.Due to the impact of the rays of the sun on the rotating earth when it's daytime here it's dark nighttime other places. There are certain foods that are available all year around but most others have their season and depends on sunshine and rain.

An amazing thing is although there are massive oceans and rivers, sometimes there are floods and other times droughts, when there are excessive rainfall there have never been any incidents where the leakage of water from the earth affect any other plannet.There is also the wind, when I was a child we used to fly kites and in water sports they do sailing and also utilize the wind to drive boats. The universe was the first creation of God, heaven is one of the planets that is in the universe ajacent to the earth.

God is truly amazing and I will make no apology to keep mentioning him as he sustains us. There are several concepts that I cannot condone and is based on my discoveries. The earth is a round globe but it's stated in the bible as having four corners. East, west, north and south are directions not corners. At this stage of our encounter there are some facts I will share with all my international english audience, and it concerns the source of our existence from the beginning.

God is a trinity meaning three spirits combined for one purpose in the interest of our existence for it's duration. Heaven is a spiritual planet and kingdom of God in the universe that's being occupied by his angelic forces with Michael the archangel in command.Lucifer was one of the angels and he defected early to become a opposition to Almighty God thereby creating polarity. One of his early act he did was to intercept the act of worshiping God by devising and implementing religions utilizing the name of Jesus as a commodity to fuel an industry based on financial resources.

The act included the image of a cocation male to be utilized as an instrument to promote his religous industry.The mental faculties of humanity was poluted with deceptions. Christ the son of God, a Spirit with the words from God and a member of the trinity of God, this is all Truth. The beginning was when the earth started rotating and the clock of time started ticking. I will inform the world that all the words from God was disclosed through the mouths of prophets and still being disbursed by mortal beings.

During that same time God was setting up his kingdom on heaven he was also populating the earth with a world of humanity. God created only two humans, all the others until this day are made through a process. When the earth was inhabited by the world, Lucifer got involved with his antics to the point where God was over wealmed and decided to destroy it totally by water. There was a godly man named Noah that was living right and God gave him instructions to build a boatlike vessel called the ark.

When the ark was completed, God disclosed to him who and what to load onto it to be saved from the flood. There came the flood and the total earth submerged and all it's inhabitance were destroyed. In a period of time the water receeded and the ark landed on a dry earth and the saved ones was disembarked for a new beginning. There were preparations being made for the start of a new world with the anticipation that humanity would have the opportunity to be safe from that evil adversary.

Jesus our saviour, redeemer, messiah, king of the Jews, a desendant and representative of Christ. Holy the spirit of God and a member of the trinity implanted a seed in the vergin Mary through the the process. Jesus was born long after that ark of Noah landed on dry earth and was not in existence in the beginning. There was no disclosure of his childhood but he matured to do the will of the father and selected twelve deciples to assist him. I'll remind you that the father was well pleased of his accomplishments.

I will disclose to you that the cocasion image of Jesus that religions utilize as a god until this day existed before Jesus was born. Christ disclosed to humanity throught the mouth of Jesus that the only way to approach the throne of grace to the father with our prayers and suplications is by him. We the world was given the opportunity to let our requests be made known to God and they will be granted according to his will.

Victims Of The System.

This is an example of how the financial institutions operate, and with the assistance of my microscope I see it disadvantageous for a natural human in this age and at this stage in time. This book contains several different aspects of life and although most of it is based on the American ways of life, there are enough mental substance for all the english world. My advise to you is to concentrate on what's applicable to you, basically this publication was designed to provide neutrients for human minds.

Excuse me for mentioning the evil adversary because I'm not here to promote his agenda but to disclose to you all the intricasies involved so you can resent the defaults. Similar to how the evil adversary developed the industry of numerous religions to take disadvantave of the limited resources of the destitute poor and unfortunate ones among us. There is a collection practice called tithing and recently I was astonished when I read of a ninety two year old lady that was expelled from her church because of getting behind on her tithes.

Presently I have more than enough people to begin a religion but I refuse to do it because I reject joining satan in his ventures. My primary assignment is to share my inspirations with all of humanity to expand the kingdom of God on this earth as it is on Heaven. I will now let you be aware that I do not expect you all to agree with all my opinions but respect and put them in your hearts to be pondered on. I am aware that we all have different belief systems so I respect yours as you are entitled to them.

Recently my driver disclosed to me that he does not beleave in God, that tells me that he is in the councel of the ungodly. In the meantime I have to be making preparations not to stand in the way of habitual sinners nor sit in the seat of the scornful so my delight will be in the laws of my God so whatever I do will prosper. This world consist of several different people, the vitally important aspect of it all is our state of mind. Knowledge is power and power is might, we must gain the joy of our Lord and be strong.

There is a multi-million dollar drug industry with commodities called medications.The primary victims are us humans and most of us are rescued by the insurance companys as they assume a large percentage of the cost for our survival. This is how it's designed, we the people are targeted by having to consume foods loaded with dangerous chemicals. Eventually we get ill and the first organ in our body that is a victim is the heart pump. The first diagnosis is high blood pressure that generate millions of dollars for the industry.

Medications are made available to curtail and control the blood pressure within the designed perimeter. The fact is that low blood pressure is more critical and dangerous than the high one. Blood at a certain pressure is required to transport oxygen and neutrients to sections of the main control center called the brain. If the blood pressure goes too low sections of the brain becomes deficient of sustainance and cause it to shut down and that is called a stroke.

Whereby certain substance that is usually send to certain organs sease causing a malfunction impacting the process of the functions of the body. Physical life is emencely complecated based on the numerous amount of different organs working in a sequence of coordination sustaining life. One of the main components of our existence is the air that we breath composing primarily of oxygen but in most case it's poluted with toxins in the atmosphere and other places. Presently in this year 2020 based on the plans of the evil adversary, he have devised paranoya whereby people worldwide are wearing masks.

When masks are worn for extended periods automatically our body start recycling barbon dioxide, which is detrmental to our lives.We breath for the intake of air to be processed by our lungs.Technically God is our refuge and strenght also the owner of our breath this is information for conscious minds that are walking the right pathway. I do assume that you are aware that the preceeding sinerio was concerning one organ and realize that there are numerous other organs intacted in each individual human's body.

The other organ I will mention as it's also prevalent and in line with the heart, are the kidneys in most cases they are shut down through unhealthy habits and practices. It have indentified that the main distruction of humans especially in the western world is smoking and the quality of the digesive intakes. Recently there are even commercials on different medias appealing for organ doners to contribute. Another area is blood transfusion which is a very intricate venture because of the possibility of polution based on people's lifestyle.

I assume that the major factions that facilitate extingtion are habits, although I am convinced that we are all on a timer with an appointment with death. The main formula I detect is called ACT alcohol, coffee and tobaco, there are others that are too numerous to mention.There are also motor vehicle accidents and othors that inpact the wellness system to maintain the existence of that industry. The process of all industries require a source to generate products and dump the waste, in this case it's the ill patients with the insurance companys as their breath.

Next resource are the human mechanics known as doctors who are the main distrubuters of the chemicals called medicatioms. The system is so lucrative to the point that there are other country's duplicating the drugs making them to have the same potentials and call them generics.There are huge and numerous faculties called hospitals with their staff of care givers called nurses.There are also technitions and other support systems, the entire process is so enormous that it's projected to be a life saving industry.

There are also moments of emergencies whereby transportation is essential to transport the victims and require drivers and paramedics. The fact of the matter is that all of us as humans do our part, in moderation until the clock stop ticking. It's a known fact over the ages that migration is healthy for the adopted country's growth. Presently we are in the year 2020 and the present US administration is setting up to commence the deportation of immigrants as they are lebeled as being illegal.

On the other hand the government of Canada that's to the north are asking to be a place of refuge based on the additional help for their workforce. There are some homeless and desperate humans out there in this capital of the world and on the other hand there are people that possess much above their requirements to exist. Recently I drove by a bus stop and deserned two suit cases, a blanket and other items just sitting there waiting for the dark clouds to fall so the owner can be accomodated for a night's rest.

There are ministers of religions that are multi-millionairs achieving their ritches from robbing the store houses of tythes and offerings. Here in the US there are some so wealthy that they travel on there own private aeroplanes. Most of them are misleading the masses by having them praying to a father in heaven and using the name of Jesus our saviour as a commodity.

The Choices We Make In Life.

I will inform you that I do have confidence that I'll be compensated for sharing these information with you, and I'm fascinated. I will share much with you as we go along, I suggest that you be cautious and careful as we all are different. What's good for the goose is not good for the gander.

This is for the ladies.

1. If you a lady find a handsom man for husband, his brain is always empty.
2. If you should find a brilliant man, he'll be too stringent with no fun.
3. If you should find a rich man they are always disrespectful.
4. If you should find a hard working man, he'll never have time for you.
5. If you should find a caring man his ex-wife will always be calling him.
6. If you should find a humble and considerate one, he's broke.
7. If you should find a responsible man usually he is not romantic.
8. If you should find an educated man he will pretend he is always right.

9. If you find an illiterate man he will always get angry if you correct him.

10. If you find a smart man he will think too much of himself and lie a lot.

We are equipped with the capability to do anything we perceive but their are times when you fail even to try. Nothing beats a failure but a trial. Always give ourselves time for our spiritual heart to ponder so we can make the right decisions, their are times when we fail even to try. Regardless of what our routine is, it's benificial to make time to meditate on the promises of God. Always give adequate time for our spiritual heart to weigh the pros and cons.

It's of vital importance that we preserve our mental state of mind, under no circumstance should we allow anything or anyone to make our life miserable. Always let piece and love abide and trust in God continually for our sustanance and guidance, survival is the name of the game. As we pursue our lives we learn, most times from others and I also acquire certain vital substance. It's my mission to furtilize human minds to cause joy and pleasure not pain.

One of which is, it does not matter what certificates we have hanging on our walls they do not make us more than who you really are. In most cases it's difficult to determine the difference of standing up for what we beleave in, and mentaining what we stand for. It does not matter how thin we slice a situation, there will always be two sides to be annalized to determine the reality of it. It's of vital importance to give ourselves time to do an analysis before acting.

Two of the main components of our emotions are pain and laughter, the latter in enormous proportion can erupt tears of joy. It's a very important practice to prioritize our routine because the more systematic we plan our endeavors is the more possible it is to have a productive outcome. It's becoming like I'm issuing instructions but I'm not just sharing my discoveries. It's of vital importance that we practice controlling our emotions, there are times when the situation work itself out and we realize it was a waisted effort indulging in stress.

Self control and patience work together, we cannot have one without the other. I can remember an incident when I had my eighteen wheeler running the road, there was a pile up on a major hi-way and I decided to follow another route for a long way at zero MPH and eventually exitted to avoid the pile-up. When I got back on the hi-way were that pile-up was I realized I was behind the same other truck I was following back there, it was all a waisted effort but was all for a reason. I'm sure you heard the saying being at the wrong place at the wrong time.

It all happen for a reason, be sure to always put God first in our lives and he will direct your pathway.There are times when it takes years to build up trust in someone and coincedentally we can loose it in just a moment. It's a sure thing that the earth tomorrow will face the sun in all it's glamor and splendor but there is no gaurantee that we will see it as tomorrow is promised to no one.There is a part of our being that is called the sixth sense, we should try not to overrule but obey it.

Our subconscious mind work overtime and we dream of situations concerning things we are dealing with. Case in point one of my daughters just got married and is having some issues to work out in her relationship at this early stage. She sheared it with me and asked for my advice and strangely I had a dream concerning that issue and experience insomnia. Because of the state of mind I was in most of the times being an author, usually when I'm up my tape recorder is up too. I have learnt that we have the capability to convert any bad situation to good using our mind power.

How it work is this, if you wait for something to happen nothing will happen. There has to be an innitiation with a motive before anything can be achieved. Bassed on that preamis everything will fall in place to complete a positive anticipation. Because life is not a level playing field from time to time there will be unusual situations to deal with and it's not always easy. When we become a professional at working things out the evil adversary behind the negative will move to his next victim.

Never accept any claim of winning if you did not gamble, there will always be a catch in the equation it's called scam and they are becoming prevalent especially on the internet. If I should ask you how many hearts you posses you would laugh at me and say that is a no brainier because the misconception is that each human have one heart and that is not true. Every human possesses two hearts, one is in the chest and is basically a pump that pumps blood with oxygen and nutrients throughout the body it has no memory.

The other heart is in our head adjacent to our minds in the brain. Check this out, you would consider someone with a good heart to be kind, conscious and caring for others right? What if that person also has a heart condition and have to seek medical care for survival, is that it? I hope you see where I'm going with this the most important components in our life are our demeanor, choices and the decisions we make. Decisions are made by a culmination of our spiritual hearts and minds and I will caution you to not make any decisions in an hurry always allow time for them to work themselves out.

In our lives it's important to be honest, this earth is controlled by nature and there are laws of nature, earthquakes hurricanes and flooding are acts of nature and when violated cause consequences. It is complexed but also simple, to the best of our ability be considerate of all other humans among us. In term of making decisions like I said never do it in a rush. If you make bad decisions you will suffer the consequences and if you make good ones you'll reap the benefits.

Do you know that the computer, oh how I love them! and horses are similar? you may wonder what am I talking about. This is it computers and horses have no understanding only memory and they will do anything you tell them to do. The horses by the use of a bridle and the computers by the use of a mouse and keyboard. The computer outdoes the horses anyway and sometimes I wonder what would we have done without them in this age of rapid technology explosion.

It's of vital importance to respect other people's opinions even if you disagree they are entitled to them. There are times when our curiocity is energized to do research to validate them. It is always important to identify trends and position yourselves to take advantage of opportunities that comes our way. There was a guy that made the assertion that by the time he learned enough to watch his steps, it was too late to go anywhere.Water is good to drink not because it's refreshing but it also help the body to dispose of waste.

Always be sure that the water we consume is filtered and purified because it's derived from underground sources and there are lots of polutants dumped there. We all possesss hidden talents, have you ever tried singing in the shower? you should try it you'll be amazed. There are times when circumstances causes us to encounter stress, that's usually because of the faulty decisions we made, don't be confused just be tollerant.

I will endeavor to caution you as to not allowing yourself to be stressed out because of faulty decisions as our body are monitored by our brains. It is detrimental if the wrong signal gets to the brain which is the body's main computer, when that happens it will have the glands dispence wrong fluids to the area to correct a problem that does not exist. These kinds of incidents will cause severe medical problems that can be detrimental and cause premature fatality.

Beauty is in the eyes of the beholder and is skin deep, the beauty of an human can also be deceiving too. What we desern is not always what we get, there are deceptions in the equasion disguised. Presently especially the females spend a lot of money on make up, false hair and body parts, coloring nails and attractive apparels it's an industry. True beauty of us is in our hearts not on the outside, what you see on the outside is all vanity. Presently in 2020 with the world in a state of paranoya all outward beauty is disguised behind masks,

Doing well utilizing all the lovely attributes we possess like distributing generosity, love and compassion are all beautiful in my book. I hope you are still with me and not getting bored, if you get tired please take some time out. Locate a conscious minder to share positive thoughts with, the other day I saw a guy who went to a party and saw a very attractive young lady and it was like love at first sight to him, to get to the next stage there must be a research.

The first time I saw my first wife was in the night time and she made me beleave heaven was on holidays and the angels were set free, on this earth in real time.The guy I mentioned in the previous paragraph was very excited and began taking her out on a regular basis and introduced her to all his family and friends. The time came when they mutually decided to establish a relationship and take it to the next level. They decided to get involved in the exploration of intimacy by spending time in a suite.

Ofcource she had to get time to prepare for the excursion they were about to explore. When the young lady reappeared to innitiate the prelude before the main event. The male partner rushed out the door, got in his car and took off, of course she got scared. I assume at this point you are somewhat confused and you should be, as to what happened why the young man ran off. What happened was this, after she removed all the artificial body parts and makeup she was not the same person he was waiting for.

He did confide in a friend as to what transpired and it went like this. hold on to your seat, he said while he was waiting on his date he was attacked by an animal. He was wondering if the creature had killed the young lady and wanted to have him for desert. This is some scary stuff, he said it was a very touching experience. Apparently he was new to the game and the friend had to get him up to date with the reality of things. Guys be careful of the game it's a jungle out there. It's of vital importance that we read potent literature in order to gain knowledge as it's wisdom and nutrient for our brain.

We are living in a time when people are not satisfied with their appearance and will spend enormous amount of money to be otherwise. I will imply that there is an area where males are doing their thing too but I will not go there. There is a case where a female by a duo from the seventies TV reality series. She started the process some time ago to change her gender from female to male.The process appeared to have been successful as she eventually appeared on TV as a male with no breasts, a male voice and beard.

She said she realized she was a male from she was a teenager and felt very uncomfortable living the life of a female. There are people that beleave in luck and indulge in gambling, yes they may win but the chances are low. Casinos and other gambling dens are designed to make money not to distribute it to loosers. There are times occasionally when they give money away to motivate activities, there are people that gamble out all their money and have nothing to show for it. It is better to cut and run than stay and burn, the race is not for the swift but for those who can endure to the end.

It is never too late to innitiate a new beginning today can always be regulated as a new beginning. My advice to you is not to allow your life pursuit to be come a routine, always confront the challenges to be progressive. Happiness is a state of mind and a fruit of the spirit, condone the components of it and enjoy it's pleasures.The future is never in a rush it comes a day at a time it's not like a bus, time waits on no one. Do not put off for tomorrow what can be done today, procrastination is a defect.

Our conscious minds are in a state of vacuum absorbing information from our five senses, never allow anything to interrupt or impede it's functions. The challenges in the process of our life pursuit is a test to overcome and enjoy the true pleasures of life. The fact of the matter is we need to get our thoughts synchronized to have the capabillity to divert our chain of thought in the right direction. I will not tell you it will be easy as it will require an enormous amount of determination.

What other people think of you is none of your business, let piece and love abide. There are people who are deceived by the evil forces and resort to stimulants and at times get addicted. By using stimulants you will be technically become retarded and awaits extinction. We were all born as a child crying and depart life sleeping, over time our mantal faculties develop in phases to function. In the reading of this book if you should see something mentioned more than once just ignore it because repetition is the adesive that attaches information to our minds to be contemplated and processed.

There is no perfection in civilization and me as an author do not have the capability to retain what have been already documented to your benefit, no apology is necessary. Whenever you reached an intersection in life, before you make a decision consult your mental factualities. I hope you are enjoying your investment in the purchasing of this book and not bored as my intent is to share my discoveries with my readers. Here we go again, in the equation of life there are several processes. Our bodies produce essential fluids like blood, urine, tears, muclous and several others.

Someone's feelings can be hurt due to the sensitivity of their mind to affect their state of mind. Our being was designed with polarities, negative and positive.Never allow the dark and negetive clouds of today to impede the brilliant glow of a brighter tomorrow. The contents of our demeanor is catigorized good, better and best. It is benificial to invest in the latter and achieve excellence. Love is a fruit of the spirit and was given to us to be distributed by utilizing generosity and compassion. The satisfaction of our desiers are essential and fuels our requirements for recouperation.

When we retire for the day and go to sleep that seperate darkness from light to verifies that the earth does rotate. It's pleasurable to interact with nature and enjoy the impact of it all as it will eventually produce nurishments for our minds. Beyond the horizen of distant shores I can desern the melodies from the churps of the nightergales and feast on the fragrances of roses and blossoms being conveyed by the wind. Activate your awareness as to the direction you should be persuing naturally.

It will be advantageous to boycott the electronic media as it is the main downfall of young minds in the name of entertainment. Start reading books with mental neutrients and seek materials to meditate on. Do not indulge in stressful situations or go back to the past. It is not a good practice to share your situations and challenges with others. The scriptures is a good mean of directives to quote from, although there are inconsistencies in it.

Christ in conjuntion with Jesus his representetive is in the process of preparing a place for us, the ones who accept Jesus as our savior, No human have ever been to heaven except the conformed only begotten son of God, and none ever will, it's a spiritual domain assigned to the angelic forces. Fortunately there are 144, 000 choosen humans selected to participate in the battle of armagidden. The evil advesary satan will always be a looser and is destined for the lake of fire.

In my research I have discovered that there is no hell where instead when the bad ones among us leave this life they are automatically claimed by satan gone to await to be with him in the lake of fire too. there will be no trace of them. This book was not designed to be any indoctrination tool instead it's a source of exposing the misconceptions and realities of life. I will encourage all my readers to seek opportunities to bless others with direction to the narrow gate through Christ and be rewarded.

Our spoken words are highly substantial and there are times when we happen to use the wrong ones and have to apologize, even if the appology is accepted the stain will stick. There are three things that comes not back, a spoken word, a sped arrow and a neglected opportunity. Our tongue is the organ we use to talk and taste but it can also be used as a sharp sword that is capable of doing a substantial amount of damage. These are realities of life and when we are aware of them it makes life easier.

This is something to ponder, the happiness of our lives depend on the quality of our thoughts. Most people unfortunately rely on material things to be happy. If our happiness relies on material things it will be temporary as the source will eventually be exhausted. Let us not rely on anyone to make us happy, develop trust in the source of your existence and everything will fall in place. Always be conscious and be persistent as life is what we make it.There are times when we encounter unusual circumstances but do not allow it to get us involved in stress as the wrong signals will go to the main computer that will discharge fluids to extinguish it.

Most circumstances require patience so they can work themselves out back to normalcy. The heaviest thing we can ever carry is a grudge, never hate anyone, always let peace and love abide, always be carefully conscious as we are being monitored by the evil forces that are awaiting the opportunity to arm us. It's benificial to do what it takes to have the security of God as your guard.When we go to bed at nights we should always say a prayer of gratitude to our sustainer and source by way of our intercessor Christ. Press the delete button and have a good night's rest.

Always start the next day anew and deal with the new situations you encounter because there will always be new ones, if at anytime you need help seek it. Be sure our words are always true with potential like a bank deposit. Never make commitments we cannot keep, some dreams are real and others illusive assort them and never give up on the good ones. If you anticipate your dreams coming through try not to oversleep, in life it's productive to set goals and consistently work towards achieving them. If you lack the courage to commence a project you have allready lost, so it's best to keep the door open.

Life is too short to generate regrets, instead always seek ways to do good in helping others in their battles of life. Enjoy the ride of your life, sometimes we are required to take some timeout and allow the winds of time and situations to blow by.There are times when we get caught up in determining who is right or who is wrong and forget what's right and what's wrong. Of all the things we attire ourselves with, the expressions we wear on our faces are of vital importance. Having a good attitude it's a recipe for having a good life, always project a pleasant appearance.

The spoken word is always substantial, listen more and talk less. the words listen and silent are spelt with the same letters meaning they are relevant.

This is meant to be a treat for you, it's a poem I wrote some time ago.

Life sure seem like a gamble.

Love is not a toy.

The best attitude is to be humble.

It's been predestined that the meek will inhearit paradise.

Always make decisions to cause us joy, the joy of the Lord is our strength.

Without rain the earth is tough.

Endurance is the key to be a conquirer.

With persistence you will get over the bridge and acquire the prize.

In the persuet of life's journey there will be mountains to climb.

Seek acknowledge as your source of existence and give thanks to God.

Let's continually jump the hurdles of life and be conquerors.

Insist on doing your best in the process of survive.

The wages of sin is death and the gift of God is eternal life.

Beyond The Bloom

This book was designed with nutients to enhance your mental faculties to suffice seniority to reach higher altitudes. The elevation to mental maturity cannot be derived at a rapid pace but while others rest it requires time to meditate to cultivate potent mental commodities. There are occasions when humans from primitive and desperate origins elevate beyond anticipated maturity. The pursuit of each individual life is unique because there are no two completely identical humans even if you were born twins.

I am convinced that the life of us all have a blue print schematic of our destiny from origination to extingtion. The pathway of life can be progressive based on the choises and decisions we make, our choice in friends and associates do have an impact on the end product. The recognition and respect of our maker and main source of sustanance including the family unit are vital essentials in the equation of living. Each of us do possess different opinions that should be respected by others even if there are disagreements.

This world is a combination of all kinds of people from different locations on this planet earth comprized of different languages, color or creed. There is a concept that all things work together for our good and there are compensations for our actions in different dimentions, right, wrong, abusive and others.

The most rewarding aspect is to be involved in this process of life with generosity in moderation. Aways be compassionate and identify distress in any degree to help satisfy needs.

The key elements that can impact our mental faculties are the capability of desernment and comprehension, it can be detremental if there is a lack of coordination. It's degrading to indulge in actions like retaliation, procrastination, revenge, seclusion and excessive acceleration of matters. It's better to utilize tollerance, patience, determination, compassion, positive assumptions and maintain a piece of mind. Indulge in the practise of meditation induced in tranquility.

There are inspirations and perceptions documented that the peace of God with compassion is a preservative for our hearts and minds by way of Christ our Lord. I will assume that you will tolerate me mentioning our main source. It's of vital importance to indulge in the process that promotes longivity. Earlier in this ordeal I mentioned that I'm a christian but not affiliated with any religeon as they are devisive and misleading. Christianity is a personally choosen pathway in the persuit of the venture of life.

The bible is not totally the word of God but it contains enormous amounts of words from God to be utilized as directives to the pathway we have to travel. It is a pleasant and joyous occasion to be blessed to the point where we can make requests to our maker and sustainer and be rewarded according to his will. I do not know about you but for me God is my main source of existence and I will continually give him honor, praises and thanksgiving for his sustainance.

Secondly it's me, I always endeavor to maintain an image that attracts respect from all who I encounter in life. I do care for and love everyone even the ones that I do not accept or condone their wrong doings and evil deeds. Eventually they will be judged and be rewarded, I had disagreements in verbal utterances and beleafs but respect the opinions of everyone. It is of vital importance to be conscious and cultivate mental products with our minds.

We were all placed here for a alotted amount of time to accomplish a mission by our maker. Never allow yourself to be distracted by deviciive thoughts improvised by the evil adversary, seek essential directives to persue the right pathway. God did'nt send Jesus here begotted because he was not begotted after his transformation. The father was well pleased with his accomplishments so he begotted him as his one and only begotted/ adopted son. Jesus was assended to heaven to join Christ in one accord to do the will of the father.

Eventually we will join them at a place that is being prepared for us named eternal paradise. Let us all welcome and treasure each brand new day of our lives with joy hope and splendor regardless of the negative obsticles we encounter. May the bloom of our endeavors contribute to the perpetuation of our lives to promote it's longivity. It is worthless to be selfish and rewarding to be humble and careing to the unfortunate ones among us as sharing is careing. There is a place called rock bottom and destitution that get someone there.

Blessings are more valuable than an accumulation of riches in silver or gold. Of all the eminent defaults we may encounter in life, volnorability is the most dangerous. Seek to acquire wisdom, knowledge and understanding to develop our potentials to it's highest elevation to achieve success. Memories are made of this, it's benificial to occasionally do an evaluation of the actions of our being as life is a oneway pathway and our footprints are irreplacable. Let us all live for today and cultivate a joyous hope for tomorrow although there is no gaurantee we will get there.

In close proximity of the glow of candle lights, may our being reflect the brilliance in our hearts for all to see. In absolute tranquility let us allow our minds to explore the intricacies of our being to share it. My objective is to promote eternal life, utilizing literature because life is worthless living in lack of wisdom. Our being consist of a body, soul and a spirit with love and affection all in one accord. If I could only sing I would be making a joyful noise unto my God with thanks and praise for all the blessings and previlages we have.

Tomorrow is promised to no one and according to the weather it may be raining on your side of the earth while the sun is shining on the other side. The true meaning of life is to recognize the true source of our existence. I will thank God until my last breath. The true beauty of someone comes from within, our deeds, utterances and actions specifies our charator.

The contents of our demeanor is catigorized as good, better and best, it is benificial to invest in the latter.

Seek and find melodies to soothe your minds from the splendor of your hearts. Happiness is a state of mind and a fruit of the spirit. Condone the components of it and enjoy the pleasures of life.The satisfactions of your desires are essential to fuel the requirements to recouperate and satisfy our minds. We must utilize the opportunity to enjoy the pleasures of life in the reading of this book. Repetition is an adecive that attach information to impact our minds.

In the persuit and exploration of my life, I was married three times and presently devorced although I've never filed any. Marrage is an institution built on love, the culmination of a genuine relationship / friendship between a male and female. A coordination of confidence and trust, a process to bear fruits of life and perpetuate it, and the development of mental completeness. All the elements of nature were given us to enhance the pleasures of our lives.

How sweet are the melodious churping of birds on distant shores combined with the sound of waterfalls. I hope you are aware of the impact flowers and roses have on our lives, they do confort our minds with beauty. In life we will realize there is a role for everyone you meet to play. Some will test you, some will try to use you, some will show you love and others will teach you lessons.

The ones who are truly important are the ones that bring out the best in you. There are times that you learn lessons from errors you made in making bad decisions and suffered the consequences. I must encourage you to keep gazing in the mirrors on your walls of life to appreciate who you are. For the last fourty years I've been a citizen of the United States of America the land of the free and home of the brave, but at this time in the year 2020 most of those previledges are being withdrawn.

It's essential to be tollerant, humble and meek in anticipation of gaining enterance to eteranl paradise that's being prepared for us. Christ and his decendant and representative Jesus will be our guide. Recently I managed to do an assessment of my name Noel Grace and got to realize the potency of it. Jesus was the first Noel and by Grace through faith we are saved from our sin debt through the shedded blood of Jesus our saviour.

Whenever we have to communicate with the father, we access the throne of grace by way of Christ with our prayers, suplications and requests. At this moment father we enter your gates with thanksgining in our hearts and your courts with praise. May the words of our mouth and the medetations of our hearts be acceptable to you, because you are our thrength and redeamer. We will continually magnify your name throughout the world and anticipate that your will be done. I will caution you to be careful as religions have connected Christ to Jesus as a surname, they are two different spirits.

The world of humanity occupies the planet earth, Jesus our savaiour is omnipresently operating both on the planets heaven and earth doing the will of the father. His primary function is the acquisition and accumulation of submitted souls in preparation to eventually admit them in paradise with Christ so where they are we will be also. At the comencement of the process all the souls at rest with Christ will be at the head of the line and we the ones who chose to be their possession will be changed in the twinkle of an eye to join them.

Jesus is a decendant and representative of God but not a member of the trinity of God, thereby he is not God. The name God and the title Lord is one trinity, do not allow yourselves to be deceived otherwise by religions. If you read the King James version of the bible you'll see the name of Jehovah the father ommitted and substituted by the title Lord. The true identity of the father was disclosed once in the bible Psalms 83: 18. I am appealing to the world of humanity who are addicted to religions to seek refuge in Christ.

The overwhelming hemphasis placed on Jesus belong to Christ the Lord, let's all exhault his name on high to the excellence of the father. Here's an assignment for you, be observant of the reality that the name of Christ is rearly mentioned in churches except it being attached to Jesus as a surname. It's now time to wake up and desern religous unrightousness and ask God to cleanse them with the redeeming blood of Jesus. I have realized that to make God the owner of our souls is a much easier process than immagined.

There are intricasies for the reconcilliation to bring the joy of the Lord to strengthen our hearts based on appropriate choices and decisions. It's best to make the desires of our hearts concentrate on the ultimate goal of achieving a place in the house of the Lord called paradise eternally. I love my God and have made the decision to keep his commandments and meditate on his words day and nights. I'm sharing the fruits of my research with inspirations from the highest power with my worldwide audience as it's reaping season.

Farming Of The Human Mind

The concept of mind farming is an innovative venture of exploring and utilizing the capabilities of one of the most potent and powerful asset in the existence of humanity. The human mind is the most potent and valuable instrument made by God. The human intellect is the medium through witch all vital spiritual communications are manufactured in preparation to be submitted to our main source. It's imperative to create quiet times for our minds to meditate on the information our senses acquire.

The earth have a neutral system made up of different parameters and if at anytime they exceed their limits there is a reactionary and compensation. Time and time again we hear of incidents in different parts of the earth where nature reacts and cause damage and disasters including loss of lives. There is right and wring, good and evil, hot and cold, wet and dry these are all opposites and have limits. Farming of the human conscious mind create a product named thoughts and they subsequently materialize to generate actions and products.

Every action in deeds do have a reaction to compensate for nutriality, we were instilled with the idea of having food for thoughts and that is a misconception. A thought is an imperfect product of the mind destined to produce actions vulnerable enough to cause serious consequences if not properly analyzed, utilized and guided. Our thoughts must go through a sequence of processes and the first place is the subconscious mind. Most people are ignorant of the facts being disclosed here and fall by the wayside of reality.

I will reinterate that instead of being indoctrinated, the information here will be classified as food for the brain is actually food for the mind. Once we get involved in the acquisition of substance to process the elements of existence, automatically we are involved in the farming of the mind. The decisive earth implemented system of things rely on the mind's vulnerability to indoctrinated mindsets. The masses get busy trying to find ways to manipulate the system confusing facts with fiction. The electronic media designed by the evil forces is available and designed to poison your minds with falsehood.

The human senses including our sight, feelings and verbal utterances are the antennas that supply our minds with substance to be processed. Society in general is segregated based on material substance, meaning there are people having enormous amount while others have just enough to survive. I will not cast blame on the lesser because in most cases it's caused through ignorance. I will imply that everything on this earth without the components of nature originated from a thought.

By implementing the process of mind farming automatically there is a wake-up call to mental consciousness. We must be prepared to follow a pathway to seek and acquire the necesseties to live a meaningful life. We were all made and placed here for a duration of time on this earth with all the capabilities required to survive. Guided by the power of the most high, we are all unique consisting of different characteristics. In the equation east, wast, north and south are directions not directives, there are also polarities involved. Lucifer was created by God as an angel and he defected to become an opposition to God thereby commencing polarities.

The process of mind farming is a technical endeavor and not everyone have the necessary capability, we were all given different assignments. The problem is that there are people with the capabilities that are not utilizing them. A wasted talent is like a buried treasure, the exploration and utilization of the power of the human intellgence is vital and must be enacted. We must endeavor to put in place a monument for progression so as not to retard the progress of the next generation.

In the process of our conscious mind farming endeavors, in absolute tranquility invade our mind to allow products of your imagination to cultivate products for the benefit of all humanity now and in the future. Dialogue is a productive instrument in the process of mental consciousness and can cultivate inovations. This concept is practical in the financial arena, it's easier to think and grow rich than to work and get rich.

It's detrimental to verbalize our thoughts as the opposite evil forces have the capability to intercept them and deter their accomplishments. Wake up to the realization that all things other than the elements of nature originated from a thought. We are entities placed on this planet with enormous amount of potential for a period of time to fulfill a purpose. It's imperative that we endeaver to identify our mission and fulfill it. I will caution you that you will see repetition in this venture but it's an adecive to retain substance.

At this moment in time year 2020 I will share my present thoughts with you and hope the substance it contains will impact your being. I always listen to other people's views of the realities of life and in some cases utilize them in the equations of mine to impact other minds. A gentleman gave a talk that implied that each name does have a meaning and I thought of my first name "Noel" just the sound of it says no hell which is factual based on my research of the truth in the existence of our being.

God designed our being to be versatile and gave us the previlage to make our own decisions and choices, some people indulge in doing wrongs while others comply with the rules and regulations of God and the system of things. At the hour of each one of us death we go back to the earth in dust or ashes and awaits a resurection, then a judgment when the good ones awaits going to the place Christ and Jesus are preparing called paradise and the bad ones go out of existence accompaning satan the evil one destined for the lake of fire.

Do you realize that all us humans came into this life crying and depart life in a sleep? Recently a very religous female in responce to some of my implications on social media inform me that Jesus and the father are one, of course that was mentioned in the bible. In responce to that gesture I asked, how come the father sent Jesus to this earth to minister and payed the price with his blood for the sins we inhereted and committed? Is she saying that the father been here as an human? God in three dimentions have never been human because humans sins and God hates sin.

At this moment in time it's the year twenty twenty and I can desern a detereoration in trends, trends are designed to be a process of digression. Presently based on my research and experiences it would seem like a train going in full force in reverse. That is dangerous for the future of our existence as primarily the information media is polluted with falsehood and scams as it's all computerized and interceptable by the evil forces. Us humans have to be very stringent concerning the existence of our being as the evil adversary do have access to our minds even in our sleep.

Secondly health is the process by which our life's longivity is perpetuated, it have been made commercialized and infested with substitutes that extinguishes life prematurely. In the news today the FBI disclosed that an international billion dollor illegal chemical substitute business exists. There are potent information that is subtituted by illusions and falsehood. One of the most popular defeciency in our health is high blood pressure and heart defeects, the chemical companies capitalize on them.

High blood pressure and the curtailment of it is a multimillion dollar industry including the cardiologists.

Low blood pressure is more detrimental than the high as it's not capable of transporting enough oxygen and nutrients throughout the body especially the brain, and can cause retardation.We are living in dangerous times as the truth is under attack due to the lack of substance to sustain it. Fear is a mental mechanicism that promote negative vibes to deter potent material as a cure. All humans without mental defects possesses five senses, all are located in our heads.

The only one sense of feeling is located in the entire body as it's sensetive to any changes of environmental abnormalcy. Curiosity is an essential component in the process of seeking and acquiring vital information to substantiate facts.Primarily it is of utmost importance that we verify what is the truth, lieing is one of the human defaults that God have on the list of things he dislikes. Christ the son of God second in charge declared that he is the ultimate truth, case close.

I must welcome you to the dawning of a new day, although there is no sun or regular blue skies in sight from my window today there is a brilliant glow projecting from someone in another side of the globe as the earth rotates and do change it's rotation periodically.We must always give gratitude to our sustainer and father Jehovah God and Christ his son our intercessor and Holy his spirit the trinity for the ability to function in normalcy utilizing our capabilities. Truth, facts and knowledge are all relevant but different as knowledge and facts have to be acquired and accumulated and assessed for verification.

There are also fiction, delusion and uncertainties that are devices of the evil adversary satan in the equation. At this present time that we are now living in the main means of communication is the electronic media known as the internet and it's highly influenced by the evil forces. It is loaded with illusions, deceptions and positioned to divert our human minds from the truth and the elements of it. I will caution everyone to be very careful and cautious as to the various pitfalls that are setup to implement diversions to impose on our beings. A major tool of deception is called religions, devised and implimented by the evil adversary as an industry from the past world.

We must be selective as to the source of the information that approaches us in e-mails and text messages. We do have to develop the capability to evaluate the accuracy of the contents. Of course we cannot reach the right conclusions if we get the wrong information. I will assume that most of the documentations in this chapter will not interest you but it's my assignment to disclose them to you for your minds to calculate the accuricy of them. One of the richest men in the world came up with the idea of the personal computer and it took off like a wild fire with no end in sight, there times when I wonder how would we survive without them.

That is just one example to substantiate the enormous potential of the human imagination. Regardless of this fact there are people that allow themselves to become victims of circumstances. It's a good practice at times to turn off the tube to read and penetrate the contents of a good book to put our minds in motion. Our minds are terrible asset to waste based on it's capabilities and potentials, if at anytime or for any reason it goes to rest it can be recouperated with substance. The heights attained by great people was not attained by sudden flight, but they invaded their mental faculties while others sleep and devised stratigies to excell.

It's my intent to accertain that you derive productive benifits from your investment in this book. It's benificial to excercise persistence to acquire potent knowledge to derive wisdom.

It's of paramount importance to maintain a consistent degree of happiness in your minds as it's a bloom of love and a fruit of the spirit. It impliments a complicated monument that penetrates our imagination with pleasure. Never at anytime allow anyone regardless of who it is to impede your happiness to cause pain or mental depression. At this moment in time I must express my appreciation to you for taking the time out of your buisy life persuit to consume the contents of this book, and hope you comprehend my gestures.

I must also imply that you are now in a none fiction environment as all of the contents of this book are realities of life. It's of vital importance to seek and acquire potent substance from literature to nourish and maintain a solidly sound heart and mind. Always make peace and love abide, music is a food of love that posses the capability to alleviate mental boredom. Insist on projecting a profile of salidarity utilizing elloquent implications to acquire respect in the arena of life.The fundamental implications of this monologue is designed to erect a monument of solidarity for putting the pendulum of your minds in motion for generations to come.

We all need to do an occasional evaluation of our being to desern any evidence of detereoration of progression. A major component to utilize in the equation is relocation, this planet earth that we inhabit is enormous.We can relocate and use our minds to generate sensetive, productive and innovative inventions to benifit humanity.

Essential Elements Of Our Being

All things in existence were created and some made from the original creations and sustained by God. Humans are the only specie that have the capability to show appreciation by giving thanks to our maker. Submission is a difficult process but essential for existence, in most cases there are resentments that cause short circuit in accomplishing the necessary outcomes. We must always trust in the Lord with all our hearts and minds and not to our own understandings.

In all our ways we need to acknowledge him and he will direct our pathway to the ultimate destination. The first area I will discuss is the family unit. God had it specified the sequence to abide by for it to function effectively. The man is the head and should submit to God, and the female submit to him. The children submit to both parents, what happen in most cases because of disobedience there is a short circuit.

Conflicts starts and the man jump ship leaving the unit in total turmoil. I beleave that eighty percent of teenage runaways are caused by resentment of submission. In order for the family to survive eventually a new and strange substitute leader take control and that put more fuel to the fire. We all are very complecated beings subjected to God the sustainer of our lives, there will be always trials and tribulations to encounter. We must learn the process of mixing the bitter with the sweet and be persistent by relying on the promises of God because they are sure.

Life consist of several processes with different equations, our lives were loaned to us and curtailed by rules, instructions and regulations to abide by. Majority of people have violated God's commandments by immitating Eve as she was deceived by Lucifer the devil. Although humanity is segregated based on locations on this planet earth by language, color, beliefs and creed, we are all connected by the air we breathe from the atmosphere. All human bodies were designed to operate in a vacuum mode similar to a magnet with the exception of three functions.

Inhailation of air, the disposal of waste and our verbal utterances. We inhail the air in our environment, the body extract the oxygen and dispose of carbon dioxide that is catigorized as a slow poison. Presently due to the false information devised to cause paranoya, people all over the world are wearing masks. When those masks are worn for extended periods automatically the body start recycleing the carbon dioxide, and that's detrimental to life. It causes the blood to clot, reducing the space in the veins and eventually shut things down.

The internet is a dangerous place to transact business as it was devised by the evil adversary, they have an enormouse amount of potentials and capabilities, there are times when I contemplate how could we exist without them. We all have personal information and presently there are some new things called scams, virouses and others so you always have to be careful as there are people trying to acquire your information to abuse it. Someone's US s/s number is very personal.

Recently I got a call telling me that there's evidence of someone is trying fraudently to use mine and they left a number for me to call back. When I called that number the first thing that person asked me for was my s/s number. I responded by asking him if they do not have my s/s number how do they know that there's a fraud in process? and that case was closed. We have to be very careful as there's a lot going on, it's of vital importance to seek refuge.

The main purpose of this media is to make humanity aware of the difference between the misconceptions and realities of life. The truth is under abusive attack by deceptions designed by the evil adversary satan and his forces. Presently the main source of promoting his agenda is the communication technology known as the internet and social media. Now that we are aware of the facts of this endeavor it is safe to share it with others and encourage them to acquire this book in order to divert.

It's benificial to get our mental faculties engaged in order to make the right decisions and choices.The choices we make at this moment in time will be essential for our being to head in the right direction and eventuall inherit the place Christ and Jesus are preparing for us called eternal paradise. If you are not aware of this, I will inform you that there are humans presently that are deceived and are trying to access the throne of grace to communicate with the father in the names of Jesus and his mother Mary to no avail.

Presently we are experiencing a new era of civilization whereby it seem like technology is moving at a rapid pace. I will advise my readers to never allow circumstances or indevidual implecations to deter or divert you from doing the will of God. The enemy do have the capability to intercept our thoughts and retard our minds. I'm not permitted to question the things of God but I came to the conclusion that the evil adversary is gone wild seeking souls to accompany him to that lake of fire prepared for him.

Be aware that time is like a river we cannot touch the same water twice because the flow that have passed will never pass again. Every moment of our lives is precious, it's of vital importance that we enjoy it all as it goes by. Whenever we are experiencing difficult endeavors it would seem time slows down, but that is not so. Time goes by one day at a time and each day we must give thanks to our sustainer for our breath and the previlage of living each new day.

In the equation of our lives an important element is our memory and it deterioriates in sequence with everything else. It is important that we analyze our words before we utter them, we never know how long they will stay in someone's mind. Always be sure our utterances are consolatary in cases of the necessety for healing, never forget the four powerful remedies Love, Prayer, Hope and Positivity. Happiness is a key to life, it makes us be at peace with ourselves. Embrace each day with our hearts filled with gratitude to our sustainer who is always gracious and protective of us all.

May we walk in love, peace and happiness knowing each day of life is a gift and that we are blessed. Now that I have tried to make your lives easier the fun part is to memorize the elements of these equations in our minds. I will suggest that this book be utilized as a manual for reference whenever anything come to our minds we contemplate. Always be causious of the choices and decisions you make based on circumstances, allow your heart to ponder them. There are people that depart this life before living it to the fullest because of deceptions and the main one is involvement in religions.

Thank you my readers for collaborating with my gestures based on my authentic researches to verify certain facts. I will continue to explore the irregularities in a comprensive format and eventually disclose my findings to you. Emblems of time signals traces of exhaustion due to trends and pace of developments. This will eventually negatively put an impact on stability, case in point although pace is a vital element in the duration of life it will eventually impede a positive outcome.

I will disclose to you how confident I feel knowing I'm on the right pathway, there are no alternatives. The commandment says we should seek the Lord while he can be found and call upon him while he's near. Christ the son of God is Lord. God supplies our needs, it's written that by prayer and suplications we sould make our requests be made known to him. It's my wish that all my readers read this book in it's enterety to acquire all the contents of it as it's benificial for us to gain knowledge to acqiure wisdom.

I am conscious that there are hatehiests out there in the world and other people that get turned off by spirituality. So I intentionally save the best for last and since you got this far it's benificial to endure to the end and enjoy your investment. As time went by we encounter different versions but there is only one fact called the truth and Christ is it. He disclosed through the mouth of Jesus when he was human on this earth that he is the only way to the father.

Jehovah have two sons, one is a portion of him and the other begotten/adopted. Christ empowered by Holy his spirit that reside within us once we accept our savior Jesus. The most valuable asset all of us humans possess is called our soul, it was given to us on a timer at inception when we exit our mother's womb. Whenever an abortion is done it's a murder committed, the first murder commited was by Cain killing his brother Able due to jelousy.

The most potential limb on us human's bodies is our head, it contains our brain that houses our entire spiritual faculties. Adam was the only man created by God all the rest of us were made by God through a process. The most important and vital component of our being is love, love God, ourselves and our neighbors as ourselves. No two humans can make love by performing acts of satisfaction. Love is a fruit of the spirit to be utilized accordingly through utterances, compassion and deeds.

He then chose the planet heaven to be his invisible spiritual kingdom with all his angels. The earth was then put in motion on a timer hence the commencement of time. He then realized that for it all to be coordinated polarity was necessary so the first polarity was good and evil.There were several polarities added and we will see them as we go along here. The next issue he instilled was a sequence of authority so he appointed one of his angels as his assistant and named him "Michael" the archangel.

One of the other angels, then revolted and was named Lucifer who still had the previlage to reside there. There was where polarity began, good and evil. There needed to be mortal existence so he chose the planet earth to be inhabited by beings called humans. God is a God of precision with various unusual charactaristics.This all was a major project but there is nothing too large for the God of all creation to accomplish. God then created wind, water air, all the oceans, rivers, vegetation, animals, birds, creatures, and pestelence of all different species, gender and all that came in the package.

The earth belongs to the Lord with all it's fullness. The day came when he had a conference with Christ and Holy his spirit and mutually decided "Let us create a male and female human in our likeness meaning charactaristics because God is invisible. And here we finally arrived, and the first and only human male being was created and they named him Adam and his mate Lilleth two living creatures implanted with numerous amount of organs and systems to process as life.

He devised an operating system in his head monitered by his brain adjacent to his spirit, mind, soul, mental heart and being. In this limb is also the command center that collects information from his five sences. Creating the humans was a major and very complecated venture and Lucifer had no capability to access certain complexities. Adam's created mate was diverted on another mission so he was alone, Lucifer did not get the previlege to be involved in the process, but later you will see how he invaded the habitation process.

As you can remember back then the state of Adam's devlopment was immature, and over time he developed to the point of requiring companionship. The time came when God made a female from the dust of the earth and named her Eve and she was gorgeous. Remember now that the primary purpose of humanity was to produce enormous amount of offsprings to inhabit the entire earth. Everything was set up to go according to God's plans and in his time, at the innitial stage and for some reason things were put on hold.

The participants were given instructions not to eat the fruit from the garden of life. During that time their development of mating desires came to maturity and Adam decided to wait on his creator's instructions. Lucifer invaded by interacting with Eve the weaker vessel and she allowed satan to eat the fruit and implanted a seed in her. Eventually she conceived and without disclosure of the encounter to Adam that process came to maturity she had the first childbirth and it was a set of twins.

Boy and girl, the boy's name was Cain and the girl's was Aclea and she was beautiful as her mom. Over time the only male human her husband Adam got her impregnated again, when the nine months transpired she had another set of twins, boy and girl. They gave the boy name Able and the girl Luluwa, this time this girl was not as beautiful as the first.You may be contemplating how did that spirit Lucifer the evil angel get an human pregnant.

Wait and you will see it reoccur but the next time not by the evil one, time kept on going bye and Adam and Eve kept having several other children in magnitude until they started migrating to other parts of the earth. The time came when the first two sets of twins were ready to mate and the parents did not want them to interact with their birthmate so they crossed them. Even by doing so incest was commited but could not be avoided as there wore no other humans on the earth but them.

Over time and ages a correction was made and God issued certain laws for humans to abide be in that area of human existence. Because Able's sister was not much attractive and Cain got her for his mate and Able got the beautiful one it created a jealousy. One day Cain invited Able to accompany him out in the fields, without any confrontation Cain used a tool to kill his brother Able. Able was missing for days and eventually discovered that Cain killed his brother and they got aggitated.

Hence the first murderer, Lucifer does have the capability to access human's minds, be careful. Cain eventually ran off to the land of Nod and found himself a wife, where did she come from?, and marry her in order to perpetuate the asignment given to all men to multiply and prosper. There was massive growth of humans on the earth as God planned it, and as I had mentioned earlier there had to be acts of incess in the equation as God created only one male and one female.

That makes it evident that the new wife of Cain was a reletive of his, meaning that there were acts of incest in the mix. Lucifer commenced a project of promoting sin on the earth in an effort to displease Jehovah, and over a period of time things got totally out of hand. In the process of proving his authority. I hope you remember that evil adversary named Lucifer, he was buisy setting up plans to defile the then world.

He divised an industry name religions and created a picture of a false god that he had them worshiping. Things got so bad consisting of sin whereby God decided to cleanse the earth of sin by fludding it with water. There was a certain man that was living upright pleasing God by teaching them of God's commandments. His name was Noah and he had a family consisting of a wife, three sons and their wives. Things got so bad that one day God consulted Noah and asigned him to a project he had improvised to cleanse the earth of it's wickedness.

The plan God disclosed to Noah was to build a boatlike transporter and named it the ark, large enough to accomodate Noah's entire family. Included in the boat would be Noah, his wife, his sons and their wives all species of animals including those that fly. It should be so large that it would consist of three floors as there had to be enough food to sufice all the occupants for a period of time. No other human was made aware of that plan of God so, everyoue was having fun indulging in sinful living.

Noah obeyed Jehovah by disclosing it to his sons and started gathering material. As the years went by and the ark took shape, Noah was very happy to have the support of his family. There was another aspect of the work that might have been more challenging than ark building. Noah was a preacher of rightousness so he couragously took the lead in trying to warn the people of the ungodly society of the flooding of the earth God had planned and got no responce.

They were so caught up with the activities of their daily ungodly living, nutured by Lucifer. Many of them rediculed Noah and his family, some threatned him and even tried to sabotage the construction of the ark. Noah and his family never quit although they lived in a world that was geared to making their lives primary persuit seem trivial. They were living in a period of time that the bible discribed as "The last days" The present times we are living in at this moment is similar to the days of Noah, and again the evil adversary is using religions to lead humans astray.

When the ark was in it's final stage for completion, all preparations were being made and awaiting on communications from Jehovah. Eventually the message came with a command telling Noah to start loading the ark with his family first. God also told Noah to start loading all species of animals in pairs, it must had been an unforgetable moment in time. From the horizons they streamed in by the thousands, some walking others flying, crawling, waddling.

All in an astonishing variety of sizes, shapes and dispositions, all trying to be comfortable in the congested spaces of the ark. The observers wondered how could so many verities of living creatures be comfortable in such a confine amount of space, God created them all and have dominion and control over them to survive. Another issue was loading on enough food of all kinds to suffice them for the duration. Jehovah God informed Noah when the flood would come so they had to sit there and await the falling of the rain to begin.

Noah's wife and her beautiful daughters-in-laws in the meantime was busy preparing a comfortable environment for the family to be in. Although the people of Noah's days were astonished at the process of preparation that were being made. Instead of heeding the warnings of the distruction of the world system, they mocked and rediculed the cargo on the ark. The rain started falling none stop and flooded the total earth was submerged.

Jehovah took delight seeing all those wicked people perish because they were warned by Noah. God did give all those people the choice of changing their lives from their wicked ways and they did not take the opportunity to heed the warnings. The faith of Noah kept him, his family and all those other occupants on the ark alive, if we immitate the faith of Noah and change by accepting Jesus in our hearts as our saviour, we will be secured and acquire eternal life in paradise with Christ and Jesus his representative.

Eventually the rain stopped and the water receeded, the ark landed on a dry and cleansed earth and all the occupants disembarked and there was a new beginning. The preceeding account concerning the first cleansing of the planet earth by a flood is vital information to the now generation of humanity. It shows the seriousness of Jehovah God if his orders are violated. Presently we are again living in the final days of another cleansing but this time instesd of water it will be fire.

My advice to all humanity that's not prepared for it, is to seek the narrow pathway to get on the now ark to acquire life everlasting. Unfortunetly Lucifer managed to excape the first cleansing as he returner return to heaven. There was a rainbow desigened and placed in the skies to appear periodically as a reminder for humanity to be prepared for the next cleansing of this earth. When Noah, his wife and family got to the point of setting up a new world they were given a major asignment.

Just as it was originally instructed was to produce massive amount of humans to inhabit the earth with a new generation of humans. And the process commenced, but there was a pitfalls along the way primararely due to disobedience again. I am sure you heard of Sadom and Gomarrow, God distroyed them because of disobedience of them not following is instructions. As I earlier promised that I would disclose to my readers my findings in my research of human existence. I was appauled at the anmunt of ungodlyness that transpired in the era after

Noah the man of God completed his assignment. Although Noah and his offsprings were buisy populating the earth, in the process of progression there were some really distinguished and authentative officials. Starting with Abraham I also saw several other famous kings and rulers mentioned like David, Solomon and several others.

My disappointment was the amount of distructions and killings that was done as time went by. I could also desern Jehovah's anger of the trend things were going in. Based on my observations there were times he was so angry whereby he actually destroyed cities, it seemed that the major default was caused by sin and disobedience. There were several false gods like Baal as Lucifer returned to the earth as satan after being cast out by Jesus with a new army of dangerous angels.

The Isralites and the jews were meant to be God's people but they were not as cooperative as they were meant to be. These were some difficult times as the entire earth was inhabited by the world. After the innitial cleansing of the earth with the flood I anticipated a brand new earth faithful, pure ond true to God but the wicked one seem to have intensefied his distructive missions to displease Jehovah. At this present time and from my location on this planet I can see the world heading in the wrong direction.

There are cruel authorities based on my scessment, there is no comparison to what I was exposed to in what I discovered. This substantiates my assurance that when the emminent end of this present system of things come to it's conclusion, I will be secure in the right place awaiting resurection and judgement to be in paradise with Christ and Jesus. I will be disclosing facts to substantiate my assertions on my findings as we proceed.

God in three dimentions have never been seen as henis an invisible spirit, but can be deserned, the name of the power of the most high is Holy his spirit and he was the main force that executes the will of the father. It's a known fact that God is invisible, religions have a false image in circulation that's being used as a commodity for sale called Jesus that existed as a false god in the first world before Jesus was born. Presently it's being used along with a cross to decorate places of religous worship.

They have a large percentage of humanity deceived whereby they are trying to access the throne of grace in Jesus and Mary's names. All the plans were in place and eventually the messege was sent out for preparations for the arrival of Jesus a decendant and representative of Christ to be on this earth in flesh. Satan and none of his forces knew of the proposed plans of God, so he did'nt have the capability to intervein in the process.

If you can recall somewhere earlier in this book I stated that I would show you that a spirit does have the capability to insert a seed into a womb like what Lucifer did to Eve before God was ready. Ok here we go, there was a nation of wicked people named the Amalekites that had made a decree to kill all the Jews and were wicked enimies of the people of God. Almighty God had identified a virgin, daughter of Eli and sent Holy his spirit to her. She was in the process of getting engaged to a man named Joseph a carpenter who was a man of faith. They resided in the city of Nazereth in Galilee.

Mary was highly favored by God so her course was mopped out, but she was intercepted by a servant of God. Her mission was to assume an assignment from God with the responsibility that would change her complete course of life. In order to get acquainted with Mary we need to look beyond any preconceptions about her that are promoted in religions. Let us ignore the complexity of theology and dogma that's been bestowed on this humble woman and concentrate on her favoratism by God.The name of the angel that visited Mary was Gabriel.

Gabriel disclosed to her in a vision that she was not highly favored by God. Mary had such humility that the angel Gabrael explained to her that she was assigned distinguishly to bear a child who would be the most important of all humans. The angel disclosed that Jehovah will give him the throne of David and he would rule over the house of Jacob forever. Mary was aware of that promise God made to David more than a thousand years earlier, that one of his decendants will rule forever.

The son of Mary was destined to be the messiah whom God's people over centuries have been anticipating his arrival. A more important assurance information to Mary was that her son would be named Jesus. Mary was curious as to how could she bear a child if she was not involved with a man having any copulation as she was not yet married to her proposed husband Joseph. The time came when the power of the most high God, that Holy the spirit implanted a seed from God as a human seed inside Mary.

When it germinated to the point where she could feel the movements of the infant inside her. Ok are you here with me? see I kept my promise, this is a repitition of the previous incident done by Lucifer to Eve. The angel was impressed at the reactions of Mary in the process of fulfilling the promises of God. There was a lady named Elizabeth and God revealed to her that the child that Mary was carrying would become the Messiah and disclosed to Mary that happy is she that beleaves.

The child was in the process of development inside Mary and she made predictions of his proposed mission as it was disclosed to her by God as things to come. Mary memorized a quote that was predestined to be delivered by the Messiah her son saying "What I teach is not mine but belongs to him that sent me" The time came when Mary decided to go spend some time with Elizabeth as they were close friends so she could be consoled by her.

Even up to that point Joseph was not aware of what was going on. The time came for Mary to return home but she was concerned as to the responce Joseph would have taken when he realized she was pregnant by seeing her as being unfaithful to him. She eventually disclosed it to him and he was disappointed in her, one night he had a dream that an angel was sent by God to tell him that Mary was carring a child that was inserted for God and it gave him a relief.

As a man of God he accepted it and made the decision to comply with God. It was a custom to go to Bethlehem to register all new born children so Joseph and Mary went there and could not get in because of the crowd of other people so they decided to go restup in an ajacent stable. Unfortunately in the night Mary started having intensive pains she never felt before as the childbirth process had commenced.

Eventually in amazement she delivered her first born, that's destined to be the only begotten son of the father. I do have an observation to comment on in the process preceeding and here it is. Based on the fact that the earth revolves there are different seasons based on the location of the planet.The time of the year that is now being celebrated as the birth of Jesus had to be very cold for anyone to sit on the floor of a stable. From my experiences of that similar venture it must have been much inconveniences but it was not disclose in the bible.

It was disclosed that Mary wrapped the new born child in swaddling clothing to make him as comfortable as she could. The bible also disclosed that while sheperds watch their flocks by night all seated on the ground then an angel appeared to them and disclosed that the child was born in the city of David a saviour who is Christ our Lord. Something does not seem right here as Christ the Lord our God already existed in glory. They all got excited and went in search of the newborn child that would be found in a manger.

The child was registered and when he was eight days old he was circumcised as required by the Mosaic Law. The child was named Jesus for he is was sent by God to rescue humanity from their sins An aged man named Simeon approached Mary and gave her a saying to treasure in her heart. Simeon had been promised by God that he would see the Messiah before he died and it was fulfilled. The next thing was to take the child to the temple. The word got out that the child had arrived and one night Joseph had a dream.

God told him that king Herod wanted to have the child killed so he told Mary and they had to take off to Egypt for refuge. As time went by Mary and Joseph had other children of their own and they enjoyed travelling. Jesus was an amazing young child and spent much time in and around the temples asking questions. Most of the information that I am sharing with you here were derived from the bible, if there are any inacurasy don't blame it on me.

In his travels he had confrontations along the way as any human does even with the evil adversary because even at that time saton was not aware of him. I hope you are still here with me. I know time is of the essence and valuable but the information I'm sharing with you are vauable and of vital importance. I will disclose to you that of all the research I've done I have not found any record documented concerning a detail tract of Jesus's childhood.

Much time had transpired and Joseph got aged and passed on and Mary had other children to help her. At the age of thirty Jesus got baptized and commenced his ministry and I will disclose my findings the best I can. Jesus assumed several titles like "King of the jews" "The Messiah" and several others. Somehow at the beginning of his ministry he managed to meet Lazarus and his wife Martha, She was a womwn of faith and found comfort in the presence of Jesus they lived outside the city of Bethany.

Martha disclosed to Jesus that he Jesus was the son of God that came into the world. During the innitiation of Jesus's ministry in Judia he encountered much opposition and hostility but he decided to reside in the home of Martha as he felt secured there.

Martha was sister of Mary that means that she was Jesus's aunt. Jesus eventually had to leave for some time and while he was gone Lazarus got ill and died, They contacted Jesus with that news and by that time Lazerous was already buried. Jesus did return and went to see the grave and there was a stone in front of it, he ordered them to remove the stone. By that time it was already four days he commanded Lazarus to come forth and he woke up.

Over time God used his means of utilizing the potentials of his angels to spread the good news of the presence of the Messiah on the earth. At the stage where Jesus began looking for help with his ministry to spread the good news of the kingdom of God. Also the means of utilizing the right way to acquire the privilages they possess, the first thing he did was to appoint deciples and the first one he found was Peter. I am doing my best to share with you my findings but my account is not comprehensive.

I will advise you to researh the accounts in the bible for yourself. Peter was a fisherman so they spent much time by the sea, Jesus performed many meracles and the people began to have a lot of confidence in him. Jesus was credible as he was a representative of Christ and was sent here by God to accomplish a mission. One day he enquired of Peter as to who does the people think he was and Peter told him. Lucifer the evil one eventually realized who Jesus was and started harassing him, and Jesus ordered him to get behind him.

Holy the spirit of God accompanied Jesus on his missions and they accomplished much with Jesus performing numerous mericles to prove that he was the Messiah. After Jesus been preaching for a year and a half he made an important decision to make as to choose who will he use to be his deciples, He dicided to appoint eleven others to join Peter. In making these decisions Jesus always consult the father for directions so he went by himslf to the mountain to pray to God.

In the morning he called all his followers together and chose all the deciples who will be with him. After Jesus completed training them he sent them out, on their own with the power of Holy the spirit to preach, heal the sick and expell demonds. They were designed to be the foundation of christiannity.They would be with Jesus at the most important time of his life such as before his death. Like Jesus most of the twelve were from Galelee and some married.

He told them that "I will call you all friends as I have made known to you all the things I learned from my father. After he chose the twelve deciples they all came down the mountain and saw a large crowd gathered there waiting for the Messiah. In that crowd were people possesed by demonds and some suffering with diseases and Jesus healed them all. He said in order to love God we must first love our friends, neighbors and our enemies also.

In his sermon on the mount Jesus said "Take my yoke upon you and learn of me for I am mild tempered, and lowly in heart and you will acquire refreshments in your hearts" Jesus told the deciples not to pray like the Pharisees do, but do it a certain way. Ther is only one way to pray to the father is in spirit and in truth and by way of Christ the son of God from the seed was extracted to bring Jesus in flesh that our father be sanctified. It is important to develop a personal relationship with the father.

Keep on asking, and it will be given you, look and you will find, keep on knocking and the door will be opened to you. Jesus did several amazing things like walking on the water that surprized the deciples, to their astonishment. Because Jesus healed the sick on the sabbath day the Phariscees dispised him, he healed a blind man and asked him if he had faith in the Messiah and the man told him, I would if I knew who he was and Jesus told the man "I am the messiah" and that allowed the man to have faith.

While interacting with some people Jesus told them.The true God is a God who saves, and Jehovah the sovreign God provides excape from death. Because of all the marvellous things Jesus had done the Pharisees developed an hatried for him and seek his whereabouts to get to destroy him. One of the twelve deciples who's name was Judas went to the Pharisees and enquired how much would they pay him to help them find Jesus and they told him thirty pieces of silver.

The Phadisees agreed to pay Judas so he started looking for the opportunity to hand Jesus over to them to be killed and eventually he did. Jesus came to this earth for the purpose of giving his life to save imperfect humans, and even though he died he conquered death. God was loyal to him and brought him back to life, right up until his death Jesus humbly served humanity and forgave many for their shortcomings. Jeses appeared to his deciples and tought them how to do the important works that he tought them to do including the act of baptism.

Jesus and his deciples celebrated the passover in the upper room in Jerusalem and at the end of the meal Jesus perdicted that one of them was going to betray him.The deciples were shocked and enquired who it would be and Jesus said it's the one I give the bread. Immediately after that Jesus broke a piece of bread and gave it to Judas, everyone was in amazement and Judas departed the room. He then prayed over some wine and gave it to the deciples to drink and said, this represents my blood which I will give for the forgiveness of your sins.

You will reign with me in paradise do this always in rememberance of me, most christians doe's this once per year and call it the evening meal. After the meal they all went to the garden called Gethsemane, Jesus started praying to God the father, it was about midnight then Judas appeared with an army of Philistenes with swords. Judas identified Jesus for them by giving him a kiss then they arrested Jesus. I will insist that the foundation is love, love God in three dimentions love ourselves and love others. Love is a vital component of our being, not an action for satisfaction.

It is a powerful feeling of compassion to utilize and enjoy in all seasons. Love cannot be re-made, God made it in us and it can be explored to cause reproduction and enjoyed by the pleasures and power of it. Joy is a component of love and have been identified to come in the morning like a fresh dew on vegitation. It's like a brilliant bloom of a flower in the dawning of a brand new day. Love is similar to an adhesive to attach vital substance to our minds with fundamental components for our being.

Be sure to utilize it adequately before we depart this life, this book is designed to be an instrument of a mature audeance so it's heavyly coded. Love is a many splender thing of enormous proportions, an institution of various factors in the faculty of satisfaction. Once the word love is interjected in a mature argument an alarm is activated in the brain. Regardless of the variety of agendas in the culmination of the mental process of the mind.

At this point in time it's my assumption that ya'll have deserned the capability of my sanity. It is productive for your minds. Seek and acquire my other books "Truly amazing Grace" & "A visionary Messenger" to gain knowledge as it was predicted that without knowledge people will perish. Study to be approved and you will be compensated for your good deeds. Do not store up treasures on this earth. Be compassionate to the unfortunate ones among us and be blessed. I will say, well done good and faithful servant and let you in to enjoy the joy of the Lord because of your faithfulness.

It was predicted that in the world there would be trials and tribulations, take courage and we will conqure and surpress the works of the evil adversary. They took Jesus to Pilot who claimed to be the king, and Pilot asked what did this man do? They told Pilot that Jesus claim to be the king of the Jews. Pilot asked Jesus if he was king of the Jews and Jesus told him that his kingdom is no part of this world. Pilot decided to set Jesus free and the crowd shouted, kill him. Then the soldiers started hitting him, spit on him and put a crown of thorns on his head.

Pilot handed him over to them to be executed, they took him to a place called Golgotha nailed him to a stake and raised it up, between two human thieves on croses to die. Jesus started praying to God that he forgive them as they did not know what they were doing. I hope you are all here with me still as we are just getting in the intricacy of things but if we go by the spiritual GPS we will be heading in the right direction.

Jesus while on the stake was asked a question by one of the thieves and responded to him positively with hope. Jesus died as a ransom for us all. He was transformed to be a spirit and was eventually assended to heaven, Jesus continually said it's the father that sent him here, he said "Beleave in God and beleave also in me, in my father's house there are many mansions one is paradise" It's his desire for us to be with him. Presently he is working with Christ preparing paradise to receive us that chose to be with them.

At this point based on my research Jesus was not resurrected from death on the third day as documented. Mary Magnalean went to the grave on the second day with frangrance to counteract the stench of decaying flesh and discovered that the stone on the grave was moved and the body was missing. Spirits are invisible creatures and don't have the capability to utter words. Jesus in spirit appear to Mary, she encountered his presence and tried to touch him but it was not possible to touch his spirit.

When Jesus in spirit assended to heaven God's invisible kingdom, he change the name of Lucifer to Satan and cast him out to the earth with his evil forces. The sad thing is that he can access human minds. Jesus went to be an assistant to Christ in the process of preparing paradise where we the ones that accept him will live eternally giving honor, thanks and praise to Jehovah. Our Almighty God Jehovah does not reside in heaven, it's his kingdom and the angelic forces are there.

It was documented that Jesus the representative of God sits on the right hand of God who is invisible, I'm just mking you aware of the misconceptions that are out there devised by satan. Presently Jesus spends most of his time here on earth spiritually doing the will of the father in conjunction with Christ. Jehovah God and Holy the spirit. God is omnipotent and omnipresent existing in the realms of glory. There are several religions deceptively giving their members the assurance of going to heaven. God did assign rules and regulations to comply with in his new covenant

I have put the pendolum in motion with the anticipation that you will join me in exploring this marvelous adventure. Due to the past sinful history on this earth with the world once it was cleansed with water and God made the decision that the next time it will be with fire. The rainbow is the symbol of that promise and if you are observant you will see that symbol is claimed and used by satan. Based on my research I have come to the conclusion that life is the culmination of a process that is impacted by our human decisions including interactions of our mental components.

A New Day Dawning

Here we go again, existence is a process with different forces interacting to accomplish an outcome. The main elements in the equation are negative and positive, good and evil, truth and lies, right and wrong. All living things occupying this planet earth are connected by oxygen for existence. It's a productive venture to concentrate on positive anticipations of the future. I have dedicated most of my life researching the realities of our lives called destiny. I came to the realization that it's all temporary, but the souls that are dedicated to God will go to eternal paradise.

It's of vital importance that we utilize adequate time to recouperate from exhaustion trying to survive the stress in this system of things. Be sure to mentain mental sanity to concentrate based on the products of the heart in order to make the right decisions. If you make the right ones you will reap the benifits and of course if you make the wrong ones you sure suffer the consequences. Never submit your mind to the concept of subjection, inside every human is an alternative prosess for survival.

The coordination of words coupled with the tranquality of nature have the potential to create a magnificient impact on our mental faculties. Do whatever it takes to absorb neutrients created from positive substance acquired by the senses from potent literature. Progress by utilizing your imagination to extract substance from your aspirations to be processed to present a brilliant glow from our hearts. We do have the capability to impact negative situations by substituting them with tears of joy and excitement.

Never you take the process of nameing a child as a simple action, nameing is similar to giving someone a road map to a predestined location with circumstances to encounter along the way. It is consequential to develop, maintain and project a glow of brilliance and splendor for the world to see your state of mind externally. As we go along here please allow me to reintirate as inspirations come to my mind and here's one.

There are three realms to encounter in our pathway to our final destination, mortal, spiritual and eternal the latter is only applicable if chosen.Time is durational and each human was alloted a portion of it, let's utilize our portion unselfishly by uplifting others. It is a gaurantee that there will be a brighter tomorrow but no gaurantee that anyone of us will see it. today is a treasure we presently possess let's cherish and make the most of it.

The best approach is to make hay when the sun is shining and seek shelter when it rains. This applies to all humanity, reguardless of your language, color or creed. Our dreams, wishes, hopes, anticipations and aspirations are blossoms on our tree of life. The human mortal life is a significantly spiritual and timed venture that's not recyleable. Life consist of numerous coordinated processes, and there are documented instructions available in literature.

It's our responsability to seek and acquire them that his will be done. Almighty God Jehovah our father rules our destiny and is lenient to tolerate the decisions we make with our minds to our last breath. The distructive element is called doubt, never allow it to determine the progress of your being. Lastly I will encourage you to be patient and read this complete book, yours truly appreciate your patience for the duration of this venture and gaurantee your investment was worth it.

Life is a prvilege assigned to us humans individually for a duration of time, by our maker to accomplish a mission. It is of vital importance that you seek and acquire my other books "A visionary Messenger" and "Truly anazing Grace" @ amazon. com/books or Barnes and Nobles book stores.The dawning of each new day is the beginning of the rest of our lives. Let us give thanks to our maker and rezent any wicked thoughts the wicked one try to install in our minds.

Let's not concentrate on the history of the past or our future, concentrate on now and make the best of each day. Better days are coming depending on our persistence to make it more prosperous. Concentrating on the realities of life, I desern a serious trend of diversion of dangerous dimention. It is essential to impliment ways to prepare in maturing our minds with wisdom to utilize the technical products being developed.

Because of my relationship with my maker and sustainer at all times I make sure there is space in my mind to accept and accomodate the inspirations I receive to meditate on and to document them. As time go by I accumulate them and publish them as literature to share with the world as a source of knowledge. The lack of knowledge will cause humanity to perish, I'm sure since you are so involved in this venture you will not mind me sharing some with you.

Two of the most intricate and vitally important aspects of our being are the decision and choices we utilize our minds to make. I will compliment you for choosing to be in this environment to acquire knowledge furtilize your brain. Each moment of time is precious, let's utilize them to their maximum potential. The beat goes on one day at a time, stay positive and aim for higher elevations. I will continually reintirate that no one should allow any dark cloud of today to impede the brilliant glow of a brighter tomorrow.

All humans were made unique, there are no two identical humans not even if they were born as twins. With the exception of the retarded or disabled ones among us we all were given assets with the capability to survive for the extent of our survival duration. It is benificial at an early stage of inception that the capabilities to be deserned and do whatever it takes to develop them to their maximum potential. All humans were made equally with the charastaristics of God, we must all endeavor to make peace and love abide.

I will reintirate that joy is a component of love and comes in the morning like the bloom of a rose in the dawning of a brand new day. Verbal utterances are necessary to communicate within limits, but silence is golden for us to meditate. The most essential elements of our being are air, water, nutrients and the winds of time, seek and acquire peace as a preservative. Although our presentation is important, absolute beauty originates from our mental heart in our brain not outward appearance.

Dominance is a selfish trend that promotes the system of things that is a possession of satan the god of this world, always be prepared to counteract it. Be always careful of your gestures and utterances, a spoken word can cut like a knife and cannot be retracted. From inception to the extingtion of our being it's a reality, destiny is the pathway in between. It's not totally up to us as God rules our destiny.Try not to indulge in procrastination as it is detrimental to progress, make hay when the sun is shineing and seek shelter when it rains.

The sound of music does satisfy our sense of hearing while the lyrical contents motivates our minds, always keep a song of love in your heart. It's a new day, we are a world consisting of a viriety of people, let's all try to make it a better place for generations to come by doing good deeds. It's benificial to promote generosity as it will bear fruits, we reap what we sow. We cannot reap corn if we sow peas. Like eggs may our hopes and dreams be acheavable in the nest of life, regardless of the high degree of uncertainties.

With positive anticipations and persistence our boat will anchor in times of storm. Secure your seat in paradise, by consulting Christ the conductor through the corners of our minds. Disclose, confess and let your requests be made known based on the promises documented we are secured by way of Christ and Jesus our saviour. The true meaning of life is to recognize the true source of our existence, I will give him thanks and praise to my last breath. Our total existence is on a foundation operated by several processes, our bodies produces several fluids like blood, urine and tears.

There are tears of sorrow that comes from our minds and tears of joy that comes from our hearts. The contents of our demeanor is catigorized in sequence good, better and best. It is benificial to invest in the latter. Never allow our lives persuit to become a routine to comply by, always challenge the issues to be a conqueror. Based on my researches I will disclose one of the processes of voluntary human life extingtion, it's called ACT and it's an adiction of the consumption of alcohol, coffee and tobacco.

Seek and acquire knowledge as it's an adecive that attaches potent substances to our minds and preservative the quality of our future. It's not my intent to be controversal but I will revert to when God in three dimentions decided to make man with his charactaristics. The first and only man God created was Adam, all the rest of us, even Jesus were made through a process until this day. Jesus was sent here by the father to do his will and be sacrificed to rescue us from the sins we committed and inherited from Eve and Cain as they complied with Lucifer.

Christ is Lord and in him we put our trust and know that

he will not let our trust go in vain. Jesus was sent here by the father to rescued us from distruction, we must excercise our faith and trust in him. In my research I have discovered that the minds of the world are constipated with the adiction of traditional religous teachings. It's my assigned mission to awake their consciousness to reality. When the earth was ready to be inhabited God had a conference among themselves.The most important aspect of our being is rightousness, we must seek first the kingdom of God to acquire it.

Please do an assessment in this time year 2020 worldwide to veryfy that most of the predictions made by God through the mouth of Jesus are being manifested. Wars, roumers of wars, pestilences and several others too numerous to mention. It was denoted that this does not mean the end, but it's time to put our houses in order. No one know when they will be put to rest, so it's of vital importance to choose the right pathway to eternal paradise now by way of Christ the Lord and representative Jesus.

Being a visionary messenger in my research I have identified a default, the teachings of religions have installed a reverse in the transmission of human lives. The bible is being utilized as the main source of directives to substantiate their mission. I was assigned to direct human minds in the right direction to our correct final destiny. I will refresh your memories that it was the same stratigy the evil adversary used in the distruction of the first world why it was submerged under water.

Knowledge have increased through inspirations from God,

my anticipation is that we the now world will make the right decisions to benifit our being. There are only two choices 1. Destruction in the lake of fire with satan. and 2. being with the Lord Christ and Jesus in eternal paradise that's being prepared as a new kingdom of God on earth as it is in heaven. The trinity of God exist in the realms of glory and not in heaven. Religions have humanity again worshiping that same false image of Jesus as God as in that first world.

They have people praying to a father in heaven in the name of Jesus and his mother Mary. God is the owner of our breaths and it's benificial to submit our spirits and souls to him as he controls our destiny. Let's all desire to be a possession of God that goodness and mercy folow us all our days. The joy of Christ the Lord is our strenght, may we all that love the him join in a song in sweet accord in the beauty of holiness to let our joy be made known. Jehovah is the king of glory and Christ the Lord is the only open door, with Holy his spirit as security.

At this point I will reintirate that every time God and Lord is mentioned it stipulates the trinity of God. Fortunately I acquired the name Grace not by myself but with the spirit of God within me. I have dedicated my being to God to be utilized as an instrument of his peace. It's my intent to continually convey the good news of redemption by the blood of Jesus to the entire world of humanity. To my last breath I intend to give thanks, honor and praise to God with all my soul. It's in my nature to resent the negetive and promote the positive.

The evil adversary is aware that a large percentage of

humanity have not submitted their being to be possession of God, thereby when anyone in that catigory pass on, automatically he claim them. I'm calling on all humanity to wake up and trim there lamps to be counted as children of God and sheep of his pasture. Enter the gate to the father by way of Christ our interceptor proctected by the power of Holy his powerful spirit with our prayers and suplications. we must let our requests be made known to him. I will encourage the entire world of humanity to maintain a moderate state of mind and rely on the promises of God because they are sure.

It's of vital importance to acquire wisdom and knowledge from potent literature in order to prioritize the specifics of the will of God in order to achieve our goals. I did make my choice to be utilized as an instrument of his peace in order to accomplish the mission of increasing his fold. The main tool I use is repitition, it's only one message from one true God, but there are several means of distorting it by the evil forces. It's necessary to be ceative to enhance comprention in the process.

Here's the heart of the matter, God is a trinity with three components, Christ the son of God is the second member of that trinity, he is original with no begginning or end. He was never born, created or made and exist in glory with the father and Holy the spirit not in heaven. The trinity of God created the universe with all the planets, heaven, earth, sun, moon and stars are all planets. Heaven is an invisible kingdom of God with only spirits, the earth is the only planet inhabeted by mortal humans and rotates.

The first world of humanity with the exception of Noah, his family and satan and his host was destroyed in a flood because of a religous system devised by satan serving false gods. The false picture of Jesus that religions use for worship until this day existed in that first world. Jesus was not a part of the first world as he was born long after the ark with Noah landed, the term christianity means followers of Christ/God who has the previlage to access the throne of grace to the father.

Jesus the son of man by Mary was used as an instrument of God, when he came to do the will of the father. Because God is a spirit and a spirit cannot utter in words, he speak to us through humans including Jesus when he walked this earth. On one accasion Christ/God spoke through the mouth of Jesus that he is the way, truth and life, no one can go to the throne of grace to the father but by him. Satan use his religions to have people trying to communicate with the father in the names of Jesus and his mother Mary.

Religions have a large percentage of the world of humanity constipated with deceptions, like using the bible to connect Jesus to Christ like a surname and it's like impossible to get them disconnected. Another one is having them praying to a father in heaven, our father is not in heaven he made it as a kingdom. Last and foremost for now is the false hope of going to heaven when they die, the aspirations of people should be to be in paradise when it come on the cleansed earth to be with Christ and Jesus.

Holy is the name of the spirit of God third in the trinity, with disrespect to God the religions of satan refer to him as holy/ghost, a ghost is the evilspirit of a dead human. Let's all sing holy, holy, holy Lord/God almighty in three spirits blessed trinity.

Revelation

Traditionally the word revelation implies an ending, but in this venture it's quite the opposite. We all possess different beliefs based on the substance of the information we derive from varous sources. I insist on disclosing some of my basic ones to my audience here and do not expect you all to agree all along the way. You might have seen some mentioned here before but repitition is an adesive that attaches information to our minds. Here we go, God consist of three spriual components, father, son and Holy the spirit named the trinity.

I will say it again that although Jesus is affiliated with and been begotten by the father he is not a member of the trinity. The truth must be revealed beyond the imagination of the devised and implimented religions of the evil adversary. Christ is the original son of God and a member of the trinity, he is the word, spirit and truth. Christ is not the surname of Jesus, they are two seperate spirits working together in one accord doing the will of God. Christ existed in the realms of glory.

We must contineously give thanks and praise to God in the highest, may his peace and good will be with us eternally. All three members of the trinity have names, Holy is the name of the spirit, Jehovah is the name of the father and Christ is the name of the son. There are several inconsistencies recorded in the bible and one of them is that Holy the spirit was mentioned as being a ghost. A ghost is the evil dead spirits of humans and possession of satan. In the english language there is a word called conjunction and what it means is seperating one from the other.

There's only one heaven and the only one transformed human have gone there was Jesus the only begotten son of the father, no other human will. Hallowed be thy name oh God in all the earth, the souls of God's people are destined for eternal paradise to be with Christ the Lord and Jesus enhanced by Holy the spirit. We all do have the previlage to establish a pesonal relationshio with the father by way of Christ our intercessor. There's only one way to communicate with the father of all cretion before the throne of grace is by way of Christ the solid rock and member of the trinity.

There need to be more emphasis placed on Christ than Jesus as he holds the key to eternal paradise. I love and forever give thanks and praise to Jesus for rescueing us by the shedding of his redeeming blood. Because Jesus is not a member of the trinity he is denied access to the realms of glory in the secret place of the most high where the father dwells. Most of the facts revealed in this publication are disguised by religous operatives appointed by the evil adversary. I try not to get into any confrontations or debates concerning the things of God.

Recently I was accosted by a popular minister of religion and I give him credit for his respect although he did'nt see my insinuations as being factual. He was equipped with various scriptures from the bible and required of me scriptures to substantiate my contributions. Although the bible is catigorized as the word of God it does contain words from God containing directives including his rules and regulations for us to comply with under the new covenant.

God issued a request through the prophets that "If you love me keep my commandments" There are commands, directives, predictions, guidance and other essentials necessary for human functions. When the seed from Christ became flesh named Jesus and dwell on the earth, his primary mission was to rescue us from our sin debt. Jesus disclosed several times that he was sent here by the father on a mission. In his ministry most of his utterances were God speaking to us through him.

For instance Jesus stated that he is the way truth and life, no one can go to the father but through him. That was Christ/God from whom Jesus originated speking through him as it's a known fact that Christ is the one and only way to approach the father by way of the throne of grace. There are several other utterances recorded in the bible that religions utilize to deceave humans. Until this day there are other humans like authors including myself that acquire valuable inspirations to document for the benifit of humanity as directives.

Ofcourse this irritates the evil adversary so he devise ways to counteract the exposure of the truth to deceive the human's intellect. We shall get to know the truth and be set free from religious bondage. God in three dimentions are spirits working in one accord, a spirit cannot utter or can it die, although the evil adversary and his hosts are destined for distruction in eternal fire. If it's mentioned anywhere in the bible that God actually said anything, its errorounous. Jesus was not a spirit until after his resurection and transformation but he was being used by God to warn all nations and it all was acomplished.

The bible was written by several different proffessionals with inspirations from God, like authors, poets, song writers and others. I'm surprized there is'nt a book of Paul, included in the documentations are personal opinions so in the pursuit desernment is essential. Getting to know the true charactaristics of God we'll learn that the father Jehovah is the executive, Christ the original son is the executor and Holy the spirit is the power. Our human souls are precious in God's seight causing other false gods including the evil advesary to be competing to acquire them.

The most important aspect of this venture is that we have to make a choice now while our breath is still in motion. The evil adversary have used religions to put humans in a state of fear, announcing that the second coming of Jesus is close and that's the end of time.Thats all totally false and that cause people to be scared like an hurricane is on the horizon to put up shutters. The fact of the matter is that Jesus is already here omnipresently in spirit doing the will of God the father.

We are now in the year 2020 and recently it have been announced that they are planning to attact and destroy Israel, Jesus empowered by Holy the spirit and mighty power of God will not allow that to take place as that land belongs to God.

My advice to my worldwide audience is to seek the Lord while he can be found, submit your total being to him and be secured. Be prepared to eventually be in eternal paradise wtth Christ and Jesus when the cleansing fire on the earth cools off.

I hereby welcome you all to this new chapter and if you are observant you'll see that the name of it is revelation. The purpose of it is to reveal the truth for you, so you cannot be deceived by the evil adversary and his religions. The only significance of a name is for identity, nothing more and nothing less. There are two twin brothers James and John, they are identical, the only way to know the difference is by their names. Watch this senerio, James opened an account at a bank with his money and John went to that bank and told tham that James need them to give him some of that money. What do you think would be the responce.

What I'm trying to imply here is that the only significance of a name is for identity, tell me who are you?. We know who Jesus is, he is a magficient instrument of God that was sent here by him to accomplish a mission. It was so well done that it made God please to the extent whereby he adopted him as his only begotten son. Christ the only son of God is the only way to approach the throne of grace to communicate with the father concerning our requests.

The evil adversary have designed religions to have humans trying to access the throne of grace to communicate with God in the name of Jesus without the propper credentials.What he's doing in the compitition for our souls is to deceive us to enlarge his kingdom that's destined for the lake of eternal fire including his million year appointed false leaders. Come on folkes and identify that trap, you need to repent, submit, get redeemed, obey God's commandments and be baptized in the cleansing blood of Jesus. By doing that you'll acquire a spiritual birth to get prepared for the new earth, eternal paradise.

Christ possess the key, so you'll be there with him and his representative Jesus. In his walk Jesus made a request that we humans beleave in God and beleave in him Jesus also, in the bible the names Jesus and Christ are connected and implies that Christ is Jesus's surname. In the previous request that Jesus made the word "also" denotes a deferenceation of the subjects meaning God and Jesus are different spirits. The evil adversary by way of religions have people beleave that Jesus is God and have them trying to access the father at the throne of grace in the name of Jesus and his mother Mary instead of the only way, Christ the Lord.

There are more emphasis placed on Jesus than Christ who is God. The true identity of Jesus is the only begotten son of God meaning he was adopted, he is the saviour of mankind by the shedding of his cleansing blood to pay for our sin debt. We all as humans have sinned both inherited and committed and come short of the requirements of God, this includes Jesus as he was once a human. Jesus was forgiven and was washed by baptism in the river Jordan by John the baptist. None of the three spirits / trinity have ever been an human that committed sins to be baptised for forgiveness.

God is perfect, faithful and true, let us all make our lights shine for others to see our good works in deeds and join us to expand the kingdom of God here on the earth when it's cleansed by fire to be with Christ and Jesus his representative. We all possess the capability to cultivate a positive state of mind to promote sanity, but few of us utilize it. The presentation of a classical demeanor exibits our mental state of mind, that attract others to the fold in God's pasture.

Peace is a nutrient that suffice our mental faculties. Once we get under the shadow of the wings of the Almighty, as the peace of God passes all comprentions. Christ is the original son of God, he was not created, born or made. He is Lord, Word, Way and Truth from before the beginning of time as he is a member of the trinity of God. Jesus was born of the virgin Mary who was human as the son of man. Based on the accomplishments he was appointed by God the father to do.

Hearts have been broken by evil deeds and soft words have been spoken to heal the wounds, we as God's people must give him thanks and praise continually as a routine by way of Christ. Anyone that aspire being in eternal paradise will be protected in the hands of the Almighty like an egg being kept warm by the hen. Be informed that heaven is not a place of refuge, it's one of the planets in the universe occupied by spirits God does not reside there. The atmosphare is not the heavens as religions teach, there's only one spiritual planet name heaven.

The implication that God's kingdom will come on earth as it is in heaven refers to paradise. Let's all make a joyful noise unto the Lord and come before his presence with singing sweet redemption songs of praise. The joy of the Lord is our strength, let's worship him in the beauty of holyness. Although you may disagree, I'm convinced that God is using me as a weapon for his purpose making a Johnah out of me. Happiness is generated my peace in our mental faculties not a luxury, it's a piece of mind not an whole.

Material things and financial recources cannot nurish happiness it can only sufice it. Life itself is a luxury as it was given to us as a gift with ribbons of blessings and mercies on it and can be perpetuated if not abused. I am convinced that life is predestined as we all have an appointment with death. I must appeal to humanity in the entire world to wake up from their slumber and enhance the flavor of the realities of life. Be not selfish in your compassionate deeds as sharing is caring, there will be a package of compensation awaiting us in due time.

Always be generous by casting bread on the waters of life as some day it will return as attributes of blessings.Each humans possesses a body, a spirit, two hearts, two minds, a being and a soul. This was all designed by the trinity of God in a conferance. Prior to that God had put the planet earth that humans inhabit in a timed motion nameing it the beginning. Jesus was absent from that occasion as he was not a member of the triniy. He was born as the son of man from Mary. It's documented in the bible and utilized by religions to project a beleaf system in humans that in the beginning was the word and the word was with God and the word was God, that was Christ

According to their teachings that word was Jesus and it was announced before his birth by an angel that his name will be called, Mighty God, everlasting father and prince of peace. All those deceptions were designed and implemented by the evil adversary to accomplish his mission. I'm not a teacher but a researcher for the source of our existence and share my findings with my readers if they do not mind. I consider myself as a visionary messenger and ask God to use me as an instrument for his purpose to activate the minds of the world in the right direction.

The significance of a name is basically for identity purpose and there are more than one person with the same name but with different charactaristics. Here in the US one of the main means of identity is a drivers licence, of cource not everyone have one of those. A passport, birth certificate of other significant documents can be used also. A name only is not sufficient enough to access an high security facility or previlage. The evil adversary have indoctrinated humans by way of his religeous industry to be trying to no avail to access the throne of grace to God in Jesus name.

The following cinero will signify the intricasy of this venture, say me and my twin brother were walking along the road to school. My name was James and my brother's John. Up came a bus that stopped and the driver instructed the conductor to allow me on for the ride ALSO my brother John, does that mean both brothers automatically became one? The answer is no, Jesus the Messiah and saviour of our souls requested that us all beleave in God and beleave ALSO in him. Based on my research and desernment Jesus and God are different spirits, because the same conjunction ALSO between Jesus and God was the same between James and John.

Jesus is different from God as he is not a member of the trinity and the bible and religions have adjoined them whereby I saw the mention of the Lord, Jesus, Christ as one spirit. Based on the acceptance of Jesus as our saviour and getting washed in his cleansing blood at baptism, we are destined to inherit eternal paradise with Christ and Jesus his decendant and representative. God is our refuge and strength a very present help in desperate times. We must stand in the path of righousness for his name sake, in this I'll be confident that he'll be there to accept us as our redemption is sure.

Although we all have sin and come short of the boundries set, unkowingly we can emancepate ourselves from sinful attributes to multiply our rewards. At this moment in time trends are critical based on the massive development of technecology. Every week day morning and evening I can see the school bus outside my bedroom window picking up and returning the children. Communication is of vital importance and in these days we have the very versitile cellular phones, and they do have the capability to access the internet.

My concern is of the next generation in terms of attaning knowledge and other essential subjects required for their existence for survival. By my observation every single child is looking at a cel- phone screen and faces the possibility of hitting themselves on obstacles in their pathway. I will assume that most of them are either talking to friends or on social media on the internet. I think that eventually there will be a lacking of retention of the material they should be absorbing from the teachers at school.

Our children are components of the future world and at this moment in time I'm emencely concerned about the alternative direction of their mentality, based on the infuence of technology. The evil adversary is exercising his powers to deceive the minds of young lives with elusions. Instead of concentrating on school work most of the time they are engaged in watching the TV or on the internet where there is no parental control. I'm calling on all parents to innetiate a hold on that process and get the children back to reading to acquire knowledge.

My room window in my neighborhood is right where the bus stop to pick up the kids, and based on my observation a large percentage of those children have a telephone in one hand looking at the screen. That's dangerous both for their brain and their safety, if there's an object in their way they'll collide with it. I'll try to make a commitment to make my next book a children's book for guidance, beginning with learning to pray as a priority.

This will be the prayer.... "Our father in glory, hallowed be your name we anticipate being a part of your kingdom paradise when it comes on this earth as it is in heaven. Thanks for your blessings by the acquiring of our food, forgive us of our sins. Deliver us from the temptations of the evil adversary the kingdom is yours father, we'll give you thanks and praise eternally. Amen". Next will be the numbers 0 to 10 then the alphabet A to Z.

Conclusion

At this point I can desern the finish line from a distant, it was not a race only directives that are essential for us to arrive at the correct final destination of our beings. The contents of this media adresses the critical eliments of our being that's been neglected due to the trends of this now times. I will advise you to seek and acquire my other book "Truly anazing Grace" and "A visionary Messenger" timely read and try to comprehend the potent substance embedded in them. In this life it's benificial to seek first the kingdom of God and all his rightousness to require compensation.

I'ts concluded that there is a mighty and magnificient power behind it all, God is the owner of the kingdom, Christ/ intercessor is the door and Jesus is the key. I will inform all my readers that I am a child of the true and living God, that is a personal decision I made and dedicate myself to be a sheep of his pasture. I have committed my being to fight the good fight, not with weapons but with faith against the adversary and his forces of evil to be a conqueror. One of my greatest regreats is to realize that he has access to our minds even in our sleep so at time we will dream dreams that could intercept our minds.

We must put on our armour of faith to counteract this evil adversary here I go again, a gift is something special to acquire and enjoy in most cases it's wrapped and tied with a ribbon. I have discovered in my research that the greatest gift was God allowed Jesus to be sacrificed, and his blood to pay the sin debt that we commited and inherited from our forefathers. Once we accept it we can have an eternal life in paradise, that is presently being prepared. At christmas time people are busy wrapping gifts to make other people happy, that's very compassionate.

In most cases they miss the main point of the reason for the season, I might be late on this mission but will interject this as entertainment for your minds. There are laws and rules we have to live by, there are laws of God, laws of nature and laws of man.Recently I ran into a set of laws I am not aware of the laws of reality.

Law....If you try to spit up toward the sky it will fall back in your eyes.

Law....If you do not go under a tree birds cannot dump their waste on you.

Law....Seek the Lord when he can be found, call upon him while he is near.

Law....You will never get a buisy signal if you dial a wrong number.

Law....Whenever you get a severe itch it is always out of your reach.

Law.... Rain never falls on a sunny day, it only falls when it's cloudy.

Law....Anything is possible in the outcome of an argumaet if facts are lacking.

It's important to respect other people's thoughts, opions and ideas although you may not agree. It's important that we learn to tolerate eachother as it takes all kinds of people to make this world. Sometime or othere there will be disagreements to encounter and at that time you depart seperate ways. Our thought process is very complicated so it is essential to seek wisdom by way of acquireing acurate knowledge to enlighten our tollerance of the realities of our lives.

I must remind you that I'm just a researcher in the process of seeking acurate substance to share with you. We were all made and placed here to accomplish different missions, it's also better to be our real self than to be discovered to be someone else. There are people who are good at acting and that's dangerous, when discovered to be someone else. If you are observant generally there are times when you will see people talking and laughing to themselves and are considered crazy. I do that sometimes and the last time I checked I was normal, you see we are three dimentional so the components of our being must communicate in order for us to function.

I am conscious that I was assigned for this valuable venture of major proporsions and intend to utilize it to the best of my capabillity in reaching out to the world. Christ with Jesus are preparing a place for us called paradise, let peace, love and unity abide within humanity to acquire residence in eternity. I'm sure the desernment of my disclosurs are visible in this venture. I must apologize for the errors I've made due to my deficiency in typing. I will caution you not to use much of your time reading story books to awaken history of the past, life is a oneway journey and by doing that it recouperate the past let's look ahead.

The worldwide web is the most viable means of communication in existence presently. Based on the products of my researches my desire is to shaire it with the entire english world. It sure is an enormous world out there. There are important information that they are not aware of, especially the destiny of our being. This was an assignment I got and sure will be compensated for accomplishing it. Thanks for your time and attention and please shaire it with all your friends and associates.

Well we are getting to the point of departure and I must declear that I'll miss your company. My hope is that the contents of this publication that I shared with you will impact your minds. I do a lot of reading and research and do not expect you to agree with all my views and gestures but life goes on and we have to face and endure the realities of it.Yesterday I explored the atmosphere of distant shores, today I am standing at the exit door with hope and assurance of being in paradise with Christ and Jesus.

I rather the latter as there is no gaurantee of enduring a brighter tomorrow, may my soul rejoice, for acquiring the hope of retireing in eternity. Life is not an easy roadway, travelling the oneway pathway there will be obsticles to encounter as deterents. Endurance will make us conquer, resent and counteract the challenges we face. Although we are getting close to the culmination of this significant endeavor, I will imply that we have encountered enormous amount of mental substance.

As we divert to our seperate ways may our thoughts be diverted on a pathway to progress. It is of vital importance to seek and acquire the necessary directives to satisfy the ultimete. May our deeds be conducive and project to the world so it head in the right direction. It's a intricate venture to challenge the system of things and acquire the desires of our hearts as it's poluted with diversities. Here we go again, God is our refuge and strenght a very present help in times of trouble and needs so it's best not to fear.

We must not fear even if the earth is relocated in the universe. Let's all make a joyful noise by joining in a song with sweet accord and let our joy be known. I must disclose that I will be missing your company but hope you acquire my other books, At the initiation of this venture I was skeptical of my capability to clarify it's complexity. On my assessment at it's culmination, I give myself credit based on my elloquence.

May our endeavors be attainable and capable of counteracting the obstacles in our pathway, we will survive and conquer the ultimate goal. The magnetic components of the love within us will generate the necessary symptoms to satisfy our desires and all others that we encounter. Rejoice, again I say rejoice as the joy of the Lord is our strength. A friend told me that he was born by a river in a little tent and like the river he's been running ever since.

It's been a long time coming and based on our decisions a change will come, oh yes it will. A minute in time can make our while but if we make an error in the decisions we make it causes pain for a lifetime. It is of vital importance to know when to run, know when to walk away and know when to hide and count our blessings one by one. The total process of writing a book is a very rewarding feeling of accomplishment, but it put a strain on the brain.

There are nights that I have problems sleeping as my mind operates under a state of vacuum. The process is like the penpelum of a clock as there are streams of substance that enters my brain to be documented. Last night just by leaving the bedside radio on, I woke up empty due to the distraction. I will disclose to you that I am convinced that I possess a passport to paradise in eternity and suggest you acquire one also. As it was in the beginning so will it be in the end, the following is a gesture for the exploration of substance.

In this process of conclusion here's the real heart of the matter, Christ is the second member of the trinity of God he is original with no beginning or end. He was never born created or made and is in glory, not in heaven as heaven is a invisible planet in the universe that God made. Jesus is a close affiliate and representative of Christ/God but not a member of the trinity. Christianity signifies followers of Christ who is the only door and Jesus the key to the father.

Satan used the bible to connect Jesus to Christ as a surname, he is the controller of religions and there's one with the name church of christ but operate under the same portfolio as the others. Satan have a large persentage of humanity praying to a father in heaven in the name of Jesus and his mother Mary instead of going by Christ. That is a recipee for destruction for those that are deceived by the religous rethric, destined for that lake of fire with satan. My advice to the world is to get out from among them and seek refuge,

I declear myself a visionary messenger and an instrument of the peace of God to do his will. At this late stage of my contact with the world of humanity, I'm appealing to you to adhere to my gestures as they are implanted in me through inspirations from high powers for the purpose of expanding the new kingdom of God called paradise when it comes like it is in heaven.

I am appealing to everyone worldwide in english that have access to social media to open Facebook and explore the profile of Noel Grace the author. It is also substantial to obtain copies of my books "Truly amazing Grace" and "A visionary Mesenger" by Noel Grace and absorb the substance in the contents of them. You will be blessed by the powers of the most high.

About the Author

Noel G. Grace
Author.

This book was my intent to impliment and erect a mortal monument to activate human awareness to the realities of life. There will be enormous achievements to be derive from it. Based on the compliance and implimentations of my gestures, may goodness and mercy be with you all the days of your lives and bloom with blessings from our maker and sustainer.

I Hope to interact spiritually with ya'll in paradise.

Printed in the United States
By Bookmasters